W9-DBQ-292

Election Reform

POINT ║║║║║
║║║║║ COUNTERPOINT

Election
Reform

Alan Marzilli

SERIES CONSULTING EDITOR
Alan Marzilli, M.A., J.D.

CHELSEA HOUSE
PUBLISHERS
A Haights Cross Communications Company

Philadelphia

CHELSEA HOUSE PUBLISHERS

VP, NEW PRODUCT DEVELOPMENT Sally Cheney
DIRECTOR OF PRODUCTION Kim Shinners
CREATIVE MANAGER Takeshi Takahashi
MANUFACTURING MANAGER Diann Grasse

Staff for ELECTION REFORM

SENIOR EDITOR Tara Koellhoffer
PRODUCTION ASSISTANT Megan Emery
PHOTO EDITOR Sarah Bloom
SERIES AND COVER DESIGNER Keith Trego
LAYOUT 21st Century Publishing and Communications, Inc.

http://www.chelseahouse.com

First Printing

1 3 5 7 9 8 6 4 2

Library of Congress Cataloging-in-Publication Data

Marzilli, Alan.
  Election reform / by Alan Marzilli.
    p. cm. -- (Point/counterpoint)
Includes index.
Contents: Voting: the cornerstone of democracy? -- Point: voter rights laws should be strengthened to
ensure that each citizen has a meaningful vote -- Counterpoint: measures are needed to prevent manip-
ulation of elections and voter fraud -- Point: money is corrupting American democracy --
Counterpoint: campaign contributions are a vital part of the democratic process -- Point: the govern-
ment should regulate television advertisements and campaign coverage -- Counterpoint: government
restrictions on television advertisements and programming are unconstitutional and undemocratic --
The future of American democracy.
  ISBN 0-7910-7698-9
  1. Elections--United States--Juvenile literature. 2. Election law--United States--Juvenile literature. 3.
Political campaigns--United States--Juvenile literature. 4. Campaign funds--United States--Juvenile lit-
erature. 5. Political participation--United States--Juvenile literature. [1. Elections. 2. Politcal participation.] I.
Title. II.
Series: Point-counterpoint (Philadelphia, Pa.).
  JK1978.M37 2003
  324.6'3'0973--dc21

                              2003011607

||||||||CONTENTS

2595

Introduction
Alan Marzilli, M.A., J.D.
Durham, North Carolina

The debates presented in POINT/COUNTERPOINT are among the most interesting and controversial in contemporary American society, but studying them is more than an academic activity. They affect every citizen; they are the issues that today's leaders debate and tomorrow's will decide. The reader may one day play a central role in resolving them.

Why study both sides of the debate? It's possible that the reader will not yet have formed any opinion at all on the subject of this volume—but this is unlikely. It is more likely that the reader will already hold an opinion, probably a strong one, and very probably one formed without full exposure to the arguments of the other side. It is rare to hear an argument presented in a balanced way, and it is easy to form an opinion on too little information; these books will help to fill in the informational gaps that can never be avoided. More important, though, is the practical function of the series: Skillful argumentation requires a thorough knowledge of *both* sides—though there are seldom only two, and only by knowing what an opponent is likely to assert can one form an articulate response.

Perhaps more important is that listening to the other side sometimes helps one to see an opponent's arguments in a more human way. For example, Sister Helen Prejean, one of the nation's most visible opponents of capital punishment, has been deeply affected by her interactions with the families of murder victims. Seeing the families' grief and pain, she understands much better why people support the death penalty, and she is able to carry out her advocacy with a greater sensitivity to the needs and beliefs of those who do not agree with her. Her relativism, in turn, lends credibility to her work. Dismissing the other side of the argument as totally without merit can be too easy—it is far more useful to understand the nature of the controversy and the reasons *why* the issue defies resolution.

The most controversial issues of all are often those that center on a constitutional right. The Bill of Rights—the first ten amendments to the U.S. Constitution—spells out some of the most fundamental rights that distinguish the governmental system of the United States from those that allow fewer (or other) freedoms. But the sparsely worded document is open to interpretation, and clauses of only a few words are often at the heart of national debates. The Bill of Rights was meant to protect individual liberties; but the needs of some individuals clash with those of society as a whole, and when this happens someone has to decide where to draw the line. Thus the Constitution becomes a battleground between the rights of individuals to do as they please and the responsibility of the government to protect its citizens. The First Amendment's guarantee of "freedom of speech," for example, leads to a number of difficult questions. Some forms of expression, such as burning an American flag, lead to public outrage—but nevertheless are said to be protected by the First Amendment. Other types of expression that most people find objectionable, such as sexually explicit material involving children, are not protected because they are considered harmful. The question is not only where to draw the line, but how to do this without infringing on the personal liberties on which the United States was built.

The Bill of Rights raises many other questions about individual rights and the societal "good." Is a prayer before a high school football game an "establishment of religion" prohibited by the First Amendment? Does the Second Amendment's promise of "the right to bear arms" include concealed handguns? Is stopping and frisking someone standing on a corner known to be frequented by drug dealers a form of "unreasonable search and seizure" in violation of the Fourth Amendment? Although the nine-member U.S. Supreme Court has the ultimate authority in interpreting the Constitution, its answers do not always satisfy the public. When a group of nine people—sometimes by a five-to-four vote—makes a decision that affects the lives of hundreds of millions, public outcry can be expected. And the composition of the Court does change over time, so even a landmark decision is not guaranteed to stand forever. The limits of constitutional protection are always in flux.

These issues make headlines, divide courts, and decide elections. They are the questions most worthy of national debate, and this series aims to cover them as thoroughly as possible. Each volume sets out some of the key arguments surrounding a particular issue, even some views that most people consider extreme or radical—but presents a balanced perspective on the issue. Excerpts from the relevant laws and judicial opinions and references to central concepts, source material, and advocacy groups help the reader to explore the issues even further and to read "the letter of the law" just as the legislatures and the courts have established it.

It may seem that some debates—such as those over capital punishment and abortion, debates with a strong moral component—will never be resolved. But American history offers numerous examples of controversies that once seemed insurmountable but now are effectively settled, even if only on the surface. Abolitionists met with widespread resistance to their efforts to end slavery, and the controversy over that issue threatened to cleave the nation in two; but today public debate over the merits of slavery would be unthinkable, though racial inequalities still plague the nation. Similarly unthinkable at one time was suffrage for women and minorities, but this is now a matter of course. Distributing information about contraception once was a crime. Societies change, and attitudes change, and new questions of social justice are raised constantly while the old ones fade into irrelevancy.

Whatever the root of the controversy, the books in POINT/COUNTERPOINT seek to explain to the reader the origins of the debate, the current state of the law, and the arguments on both sides. The goal of the series is to inform the reader about the issues facing not only American politicians, but all of the nation's citizens, and to encourage the reader to become more actively involved in resolving these debates, as a voter, a concerned citizen, a journalist, an activist, or an elected official. Democracy is based on education, and every voice counts—so every opinion must be an informed one.

———————•—————————•—————————•———————

This volume examines an issue at the heart of American democracy: voting. Americans have fought hard to ensure that most adults have the right to vote: Amendments to the U.S. Constitution have extended the right to former slaves, women, and 18-year-olds. But does every vote really count? The 2000 presidential election shook the nation's faith in its electoral system. In one of the tightest races in history, Florida election workers created a national controversy by turning people away from the polls and disqualifying many of the ballots cast. Ultimately, the U.S. Supreme Court rejected Democrat Al Gore's challenge, paving the way for the inauguration of George W. Bush. In the years since the election, America's political parties have debated whether the right to vote needs stronger protection. Many people have also begun to question how political campaigns are conducted, charging that money has corrupted the process and that candidates ignore the real issues of the day and rely instead on "smear" campaigns. Until these issues are resolved, the future of American democracy will remain in doubt.

Voting: The Cornerstone of Democracy?

November 7, 2000, was Election Day in Florida, as it was all over the nation. Florida promised to be a key battleground in the presidential race between Republican Governor George W. Bush of Texas and Democratic Vice President Al Gore. With its growing population, Florida would provide a significant number of votes in the Electoral College, a group of people chosen by the states to elect the president. Whoever won Florida would receive 25 electoral votes out of 538; only California, New York, and Texas had more electoral votes. Additionally, the race in Florida promised to be close; the Democrats and Republicans had split the last two presidential elections in Florida.

On this important day, Roberta Tucker of Tallahassee was on her way to exercise her right to vote. What happened next to this African-American resident of the state capital attracted national attention. On the main road leading to a polling place in a heavily African-American voting district, a group of five Florida Highway Patrol (FHP) officers—all of them white—had set up a roadblock to stop passing cars. Though FHP officials later explained that the purpose of the roadblock was to check vehicles for faulty equipment, such as burnt-out headlights, Tucker thought there was a different reason. According to a report prepared by the U.S. Commission on Civil Rights:

> One of the troopers approached Ms. Tucker's car, asked for her driver's license, and after looking at it, returned it to her and allowed her to proceed. Ms. Tucker considered the trooper's actions to be "suspicious" because "nothing was checked, my lights, signals, or anything that [the police] usually check." . . . She also recalled being "curious" about the checkpoint because she had never seen a checkpoint at this location. Ms. Tucker added that she felt "intimidated" because "it was an Election Day and it was a big election and there were only white officers there and like I said, they didn't ask me for anything else, so I was suspicious at that."[1]

The troopers had not received official permission to conduct this roadblock, and Florida's attorney general later acknowledged, "[A] checkpoint on that date, Election Day, was absolutely not necessary for law enforcement purposes. . . ."[2] Although the troopers' actions did not prevent Tucker from voting, to many people the unauthorized roadblock signaled another act in a long line of efforts to "disenfranchise" African Americans and other minorities—meaning to prevent them from voting.

- **Do you think that it is fair for police officers to stop cars to check for identification? Do you think that it is fair to do it on Election Day?**

Election Day 2000 and Its Aftermath

Tucker's experience with the roadblock was largely overshadowed by widespread confusion and controversy throughout Florida on that fateful Election Day. In a nation in which voter turnout is already poor and faith in government is weak, what happened in Florida that day led many people in the country to completely lose faith in the electoral system and become convinced more than ever that their votes do not count. Countless Floridians were turned away from the polls because their registrations had been misplaced or their names had been misspelled on the voter rolls. Among those who did vote, malfunctioning punch-card machines and confusing ballots left many Floridians wondering whether they had really voted for the candidate of their choice.

> • **How often do people misspell your name? What if your rights were taken away every time it happened?**

As Election Day ended across the country, the race was so close that the electoral votes in Florida would prove to provide the margin of victory for either Bush or Gore. Puzzled Americans watched as the news media declared that Gore had won Florida's electoral votes, but then changed their conclusion and declared Bush the winner. With each candidate claiming to have been the rightful victor, and weeks of confusion, it would ultimately take the U.S. Supreme Court to settle the dispute, making George W. Bush the forty-third president of the United States.

On Election Night, the media had initially predicted that Gore had won the election in Florida because news sources base their predictions on "exit polls"—asking people leaving the polls which candidate they had selected. Generally, these polls are fairly accurate because people have no real reason to lie when asked. However, in Florida that night, the exit polls were misleading; because of problems with some of the ballots used, many people either voted for the wrong candidate or did not vote for any candidate.

• **Because of the time difference, the presidential election ends earlier on the East Coast than it does on the West Coast. Should people on the West Coast wait to see how their candidate did in the East before voting?**

There is no standard method of voting in the United States. Some places use voting machines in which people pull a lever next to the name of the candidate of their choice. Other places use "bubble sheets," similar to those used for standardized tests. Many places in Florida use punch cards, which required voters to punch out a small piece of paper (or "chad") to vote for a candidate.

In Florida, local election officials determined the method of voting to be used in each individual polling place. Some of those choices proved to be extremely controversial, and—many Democrats believe—ultimately cost Al Gore the presidency. The most controversial ballot was the "butterfly ballot" used in Palm Beach County. Gore had expected to do well in the county, and exit polls confirmed his confidence. As votes were tallied, though, Gore did much worse than expected, and Reform Party candidate Pat Buchanan made a surprisingly strong showing.

Why the unexpected results? Many blame the ballot. To vote for president using the butterfly ballot, the voter selected a circle from a vertical column in the middle of the ballot. On either side of the column of circles, the candidates were listed, with arrows pointing to the corresponding circle. However, many felt that the ballot was confusing. On the left-hand side of the page, the first candidate listed was Bush, and the second candidate listed was Gore. Voters for Bush needed only to select the first circle. However, Gore supporters had to be alert enough to notice that Gore's circle was the *third* one down; on the right-hand side of the page, Pat Buchanan was listed at the top, and his arrow pointed to the second circle down. Anyone who selected the second circle thinking that he or she was voting for Gore was really voting for Buchanan.

As the media began to explain its theory that Buchanan's

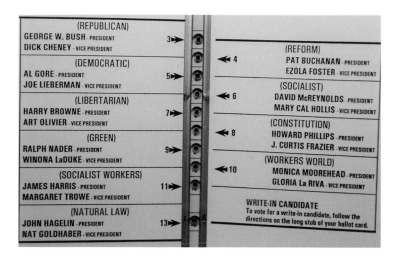

The layout of the so-called butterfly ballot (seen here) used in some places for the November 2000 presidential election may have led some confused voters to cast their votes for Reform Party candidate Pat Buchanan rather than Democrat Al Gore.

unexpected showing in Palm Beach County was due to the erroneous votes of Gore supporters, a number of Gore supporters in the county clamored to have their votes corrected. However, because the balloting was done anonymously, there was no way to confirm whether people had voted "correctly" or "incorrectly." Even without that obstacle, an even more important question was how to distinguish whether someone had voted for Buchanan and then changed his or her mind.

- **Was there any fair way to resolve the "butterfly ballot" controversy? Do you blame the government or the voters themselves?**

Palm Beach was not the only Florida county in which the ballots were called into question. Many voting precincts across the state used punch-card ballots, which register votes when someone completely pushes out the chad next to the candidate's name. As people across the nation soon learned, however, sometimes voters do not completely push out the chad. In the weeks following the election, with both Gore and Bush claiming victory in Florida, the state began a recount of its ballots. Newspapers and television covered the recount extensively, and Americans learned about "hanging chads" and "dimpled chads."

Cooped up in rooms across Florida, groups of people examined punch-card ballots. Sometimes the voter's choice was clear, but other times the choice was not so clear. The recount teams were faced with trying to decide how to count hanging chads, which were detached at one or more corners but not completely punched out. Even more problematic was the dimpled chad (or "pregnant chad"), which bulged and appeared to have been pressed, but was not detached from the ballot. The nation watched with anxious curiosity as news programs showed evaluators holding ballots up to the light or peering at them through magnifying glasses. Ultimately, in a controversial decision, the U.S. Supreme Court halted the recount, because there were no "specific standards" for determining the "intent of the voter." [3]

> • **Does it make sense to have a rule that "chads" have to be pushed out completely? Would a voter who really cared about the election leave a dimpled chad? What about a hanging chad?**

Does Every Vote Count?

Despite the fact that more than 100 million people voted in the presidential election, critics charge that the nine members of the Supreme Court elected the president with a 5–4 vote. The reason that the events of Election Day 2000 were shocking to so many people is that voting is supposed to be the cornerstone of American democracy. The right to vote for almost everyone over the age of 18 secures the freedoms of what we believe to be the most open and democratic nation in the world. The presidential election had the potential to increase participation in democracy. Many people fail to vote, figuring that "one vote doesn't make a difference." Yet, it was George W. Bush's slim margin of victory in Florida that decided the election. Had more Gore supporters voted—and many registered voters did not vote—Al Gore might have become president. The close election should have served as a lesson that every vote *does* count.

Instead, the lesson was wasted. Rather than thinking that their votes were important, many Floridians felt that their votes were useless. Many people, like journalist Neal Peirce, criticize America's "abysmal voter turnouts," which he reports are "138th in the world, sandwiched between Botswana and Chad"—two African nations.[4] The problem of low voter turnout is especially perplexing, given how hard Americans have fought for the right to vote—a right once reserved for white male landowners. As a result of amendments to the U.S. Constitution, minorities won the right to vote in 1870, women in 1920, and 18-year-olds in

FROM THE BENCH

U.S. Supreme Court Halts Florida Recount

Much of the controversy seems to revolve around ballot cards designed to be perforated by a stylus but which, either through error or deliberate omission, have not been perforated with sufficient precision for a machine to count them. In some cases a piece of the card—a chad—is hanging, say by two corners. In other cases there is no separation at all, just an indentation.

The Florida Supreme Court has ordered that the intent of the voter be discerned from such ballots. For purposes of resolving the equal protection challenge, it is not necessary to decide whether the Florida Supreme Court had the authority under the legislative scheme for resolving election disputes to define what a legal vote is and to mandate a manual recount implementing that definition. The recount mechanisms implemented in response to the decisions of the Florida Supreme Court do not satisfy the minimum requirement for non-arbitrary treatment of voters necessary to secure the fundamental right. Florida's basic command for the count of legally cast votes is to consider the "intent of the voter." ...This is unobjectionable as an abstract proposition and a starting principle. The problem inheres in the absence of specific standards to ensure its equal application....

1971. All of these amendments required dedicated and organized protest, yet today voter participation often hovers at around 50 percent.

Why is voter turnout so low? Many people believe that the American electoral system is badly damaged. Experiences like Roberta Tucker's demonstrate that some people still do not feel like they can vote without fear. Yet, the news carries reports of dogs voting, dead people voting, even *dead dogs* voting. Giant corporations, such as Enron, make headlines for widespread accounting fraud or other forms of wrongdoing, and the media reveals that these corporations have contributed enormous sums of money to elected officials for their re-election campaigns. This raises the question: Do corporations "own" Congress? Perhaps people lose interest in voting after watching months of

The want of those rules here has led to unequal evaluation of ballots in various respects. . . . Should a county canvassing board count or not count a "dimpled chad" where the voter is able to successfully dislodge the chad in every other contest on that ballot? Here, the county canvassing boards disagree. . . . As seems to have been acknowledged at oral argument, the standards for accepting or rejecting contested ballots might vary not only from county to county but indeed within a single county from one recount team to another. . . .

Palm Beach County, for example, began the process with a 1990 guideline which precluded counting completely attached chads, switched to a rule that considered a vote to be legal if any light could be seen through a chad, changed back to the 1990 rule, and then abandoned any pretense of a per se rule, only to have a court order that the county consider dimpled chads legal. This is not a process with sufficient guarantees of equal treatment. . . .

The recount process, in its features here described, is inconsistent with the minimum procedures necessary to protect the fundamental right of each voter. . . .

Source: *Bush* v. *Gore*, No. 00-949 (December 12, 2000) (per curiam).

STATE	2000 VAP	2000 REG	% REG of VAP	TURNOUT*	% TO of REG	% TO of VAP
California	24,873,000	15,707,307	63.2	10,965,822	69.8	44.1
District of Columbia	411,000	354,410	86.2	201,894	57.0	49.1
Florida	11,774,000	8,752,717	74.3	5,963,110	68.1	50.6
Illinois	8,983,000	7,129,026	79.4	4,742,115	66.5	52.8
Louisiana	3,255,000	2,730,380	83.9	1,765,656	64.7	54.2
Massachusetts	4,749,000	4,008,796	84.4	2,734,006	68.2	57.6
Michigan	7,358,000	6,861,342	93.3	4,232,501	61.7	57.5
New York	13,805,000	11,262,816	81.6	6,960,215	61.8	50.4
Ohio	8,433,000	7,537,822	89.4	4,701,998	62.4	55.8
Pennsylvania	9,155,000	7,781,997	85.0	4,912,185	63.1	53.7
Texas	14,850,000	10,267,639	69.1	6,407,037	62.4	43.1
Virginia	5,263,000	3,770,273	71.6	2,789,808	74.0	53.0
Washington	4,368,000	3,335,714	76.4	2,487,433	74.6	56.9
UNITED STATES	205,815,000	156,421,311	76.0	105,586,274	67.5	51.3

2000 VAP refers to the total Voting Age Population of the state as reported by the Bureau of Census. Please note that the VAP includes all persons over the age of 18—including a significant number of people not able to vote in U.S. elections.

2000 REG refers to the total number of registered voters as reported by the states.

* TURNOUT in this instance refers to the total vote cast for the highest office on the ballot in 2000 (president). These figures may be inconsistent with other reported turnout figures since research suggests that approximately 2% of voters fail to vote for the highest office on a fairly consistent basis.

Registration and turnout statistics courtesy of State Election Offices.

In recent years, voter turnout has generally been low, even for major national elections. This table illustrates voter registration and turnout for selected states in the election of 2000. VAP refers to the total voting age population of the state, or all people over the age of 18. REG refers to the total number of registered voters reported by each state.

advertisements attacking the candidates. They may begin to wonder whether *anyone* is worth voting for.

Election Day 2000 served as a flashpoint for problems that have been smoldering for years. There has been a flurry of legislation since the 2000 election, both at the federal level and in states around the nation. Few people are satisfied, however. Some think that further reforms are needed to ensure that every person has the right to have his or her vote counted.

> • **Have you heard people use the idea that "one vote doesn't make a difference" as an excuse for not voting? What if everyone used that excuse?**

Florida experienced widespread problems on Election Day 2000. Civil rights groups accused law enforcement of trying to prevent minorities from voting, and many people were turned away at the polls. Most significantly, thousands of ballots were called into question because the outdated and ineffective punch cards did not indicate a clear choice for president. Without the questionable ballots, the election was too close to call, and when it became clear that the close election in Florida would determine who would become the nation's next president, a statewide recount began to try to interpret the questionable ballots. Ultimately, the Supreme Court decided that the recount must stop, leading many to wonder whether every vote really does count.

Voter Rights Laws Should Be Strengthened to Ensure That Each Citizen Has a Meaningful Vote

For many civil rights activists, the events in Florida during the 2000 election were a warning sign that the voting rights of African Americans and other minorities were once again facing grave threats. Widespread disqualification of ballots signaled a reversal of over three decades of progress in enforcing each citizen's right to vote. Laws are in a constant state of change, sometimes because circumstances change, and sometimes because people find new ways of violating the laws. Throughout the history of federal voting rights legislation, there has been a constant need to strengthen laws as people found new ways to violate other people's rights.

Although the Fifteenth Amendment, ratified in 1870, declared that citizens' right to vote could not be abridged based on race or color, blatant discrimination was still alive and well nearly a century later in Mississippi and elsewhere in the South. Sometimes the registrars refused to allow people to register. Other times, people used threats or other forms of retribution—such as employers firing African Americans who had registered to vote—to discourage minorities from registering and voting. Several civil rights organizations declared 1964 the "Freedom Summer" and sent armies of young civil rights workers to the South to help put an end to the discrimination.

The civil rights workers met with a chilly reception, facing the same threats and intimidation used to discourage minorities from voting. Gangs of thugs sometimes attacked the workers. The violence reached its peak on June 20, 1964, when three civil rights workers were murdered shortly after being released from jail. They had been arrested on questionable charges while investigating the burning of a church.

The Federal Bureau of Investigation (FBI)'s "Mississippi Burning" investigation uncovered a plot that involved local law enforcement and the Ku Klux Klan (KKK), but it also brought to light the many indignities that African Americans faced on a daily basis. During the course of the investigation, agents discovered "additional situations involving alleged violations of the Civil Rights Statute concerning victims other than the three murder victims," concluding: "[T]here appeared to be a conspiracy on the part of the prime suspects; namely, the Sheriff, his Deputy, and others who are closely associated with the Sheriff's Office . . . to deprive the colored population of their civil rights."[5]

The murders of the three young men brought national attention to voting rights and spurred Congress to act. In 1965, Congress passed the Voting Rights Act,[6] which prohibited states from using written tests, "moral character" standards, or "poll taxes"—payments required in order to vote—as ways of excluding otherwise eligible voters. Congress had

Minorities in the United States, particularly women and African Americans, struggled for many years to win the right to vote, one of the most cherished rights of American citizens. In this March 1965 photograph, a group of civil rights activists led by Martin Luther King, Jr., marches to the Alabama state capital in a demonstration aimed to encourage voter registration.

found that some states used such tactics as methods for reducing the number of minority voters. The act also prohibited anyone—state official or not—from using "intimidation, threats, or coercion" to prevent people from voting. However, the law did not prohibit the bureaucracy, or "red tape," that in many states made registering to vote difficult for everyone.

> • Is it fair to compare what happened in Florida in 2000 to what happened in Mississippi during the 1960s? What similarlties are there?

The National Voter Registration Act of 1993,[7] commonly called the "Motor Voter" law, required states to make registering to vote much easier by increasing the number of places at which people could register. The law earned its nickname by requiring that states allow people to register to vote when they receive or renew a driver's license. The law also requires states to provide voter registration at public assistance ("welfare") offices, as well as many other state government offices, such as those issuing hunting and fishing licenses.

In the aftermath of widespread confusion during the 2000 election, Congress passed the Help America Vote Act[8] in 2002. In response to criticisms that voters were being turned away from the polls, the law requires states to implement "provisional balloting." This is a system in which people whose registration status cannot be verified are allowed to cast a provisional ballot, which is kept separate from other ballots. If the voter's registration status can be verified later, then the vote will count. The system will therefore cause some delay in determining the outcome of close races as election officials verify the status of any provisional ballots collected.

However, despite the passage of these voter rights laws, many people feel that the laws on the books do not do enough to protect the rights of every eligible adult citizen to vote. Even today, it is feared that many people will continue to have their efforts to register rebuffed, that they will be turned away at the polls, or that they will have their ballots discarded. Despite the many state and federal laws designed to protect voting rights, many people believe that there continue to be systematic efforts to disenfranchise minorities, immigrants, and other targeted

THE LETTER OF THE LAW

Help America Vote Act, § 303.

(a) Computerized Statewide Voter Registration List Requirements.—...

  (5) Verification of voter registration information.—

    (A) Requiring provision of certain information by applicants.—

      (i) In general.—Except as provided in clause (ii), notwithstanding any other provision of law, an application for voter registration for an election for Federal office may not be accepted or processed by a State unless the application includes—

        (I) in the case of an applicant who has been issued a current and valid driver's license, the applicant's driver's license number; or

        (II) in the case of any other applicant (other than an applicant to whom clause (ii) applies), the last 4 digits of the applicant's social security number.

      (ii) Special rule for applicants without driver's license or social security number.—If an applicant for voter registration for an election for Federal office has not been issued a current and valid driver's license or a social security number, the State shall assign the applicant a number which will serve to identify the applicant for voter registration purposes....

      (iii) Determination of validity of numbers provided.—The State shall determine whether the information provided by an individual is sufficient to meet the requirements of this subparagraph, in accordance with State law....

(b) Requirements for Voters Who Register by Mail.—

  (1) In general.—... [A] State shall, in a uniform and nondiscriminatory manner, require an individual to meet the requirements of paragraph (2) if—

    (A) the individual registered to vote in a jurisdiction by mail; and

groups. Critics charge that the laws on the books are either ignored or manipulated as the "powers that be" find new ways to skirt these laws.

> • Why do you think that Congress has had so much trouble passing a law that effectively deals with voter disenfranchisement?

(B) (i) the individual has not previously voted in an election for Federal office in the State; or
   (ii) the individual has not previously voted in such an election in the jurisdiction and the jurisdiction is located in a State that does not have a computerized list that complies with the requirements of subsection (a).

(2) Requirements.—
   (A) In general.—An individual meets the requirements of this paragraph if the individual—
      (i) in the case of an individual who votes in person—
      (I) presents to the appropriate State or local election official a current and valid photo identification; or
      (II) presents to the appropriate State or local election official a copy of a current utility bill, bank statement, government check, paycheck, or other government document that shows the name and address of the voter. . . .
   (B) Fail-safe voting.—
      (i) In person.—An individual who desires to vote in person, but who does not meet the requirements of subparagraph (A)(i), may cast a provisional ballot under section 302(a). . . .

(4) Contents of mail-in registration form.—
   (A) In general.—The mail voter registration form . . . shall include the following:
      (i) The question "Are you a citizen of the United States of America?" and boxes for the applicant to check to indicate whether the applicant is or is not a citizen of the United States.

Source: Help America Vote Act, 42 U.S.C. § 15483

Barriers to voting disproportionately affect immigrants, minorities, and the poor.

Over the years, disenfranchisement of minorities has taken many forms. Since the ratification of the Fifteenth Amendment in 1870, it had been illegal for states to deny people the right to vote based on their race. However, the events leading up to the passage of the Voting Rights Act had made it clear that some state officials and private citizens were determined to keep minorities from voting. Although today, outright discrimination is illegal, many civil rights groups have shifted their focus on barriers to registration and voting, as many of these disproportionately affect immigrants, minorities, and the poor.

It is likely that some problems on Election Day are unavoidable. Most of the people staffing the polls are not full-time election workers; rather, they are hired for the day to work at the polls. People are supposed to vote in a designated precinct, which can change when people move, even if they move a short distance. Purchasing new voting equipment is usually not a priority for states, which have many other financial obligations. When filling out ballots, some human error is unavoidable, and it is likely that there also will be errors when tabulating millions of votes.

> • **Is there a difference between acts of deliberate discrimination and legitimate actions that have a disproportionate effect on minorities?**

Though 100 percent voting accuracy might not be achievable, many people think that the states can do a better job each Election Day. Furthermore, many would like to see improvements made so that every voting precinct—whether it is in a wealthy suburb, an inner-city neighborhood, or a poor rural county—is equally good, or at least equally mediocre. When it comes to voting errors that lead to votes not being counted, it appears that minorities and the poor seem to bear the brunt of the problem. In its review of the 2000 election in Florida, the U.S. Commission on Civil Rights concluded: "African Americans

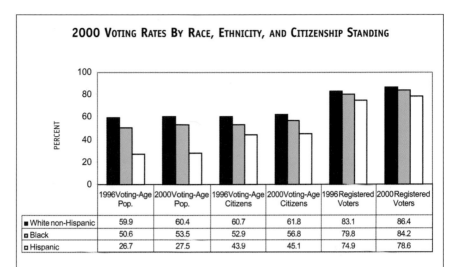

2000 VOTING RATES BY RACE, ETHNICITY, AND CITIZENSHIP STANDING

	1996 Voting-Age Pop.	2000 Voting-Age Pop.	1996 Voting-Age Citizens	2000 Voting-Age Citizens	1996 Registered Voters	2000 Registered Voters
■ White non-Hispanic	59.9	60.4	60.7	61.8	83.1	86.4
▫ Black	50.6	53.5	52.9	56.8	79.8	84.2
▫ Hispanic	26.7	27.5	43.9	45.1	74.9	78.6

Source: U.S. Census Bureau, *Voting and Registration in the Election of November 2000*, Table A. Reported Voting and Registration by Citizenship, Race and Hispanic Origin: November 1996 and 2000, issued February 2002.

Many people argue that the lack of voting rights is particularly prevalent among minorities. Traditionally, African-American and Hispanic voter turnout has been lower than it is for whites. This chart, which compares voting rates by race and citizenship in the years 1996 and 2000, shows how voting rates have become slightly closer among the races in recent years.

were nearly 10 times more likely than white voters to have their ballots rejected in the November 2000 election."[9]

• What factors might lead to an increase in voting problems in poorer communities?

The commission attributed the disproportionate effect on minorities to the use of outdated equipment—such as punch-card machines—in counties with large minority populations:

For example, in Gadsden County, the only county in the state with an African American majority, approximately one in eight voters was disenfranchised. In Leon County, on the other hand, which is home to the prosperous state capital and two state universities, fewer than two votes in 1,000 were not counted. In Florida, of the 100 precincts with the highest numbers of disqualified ballots, 83 of them are majority-black precincts.[10]

Such problems were not unique to Florida. Noting at a congressional hearing that, in her home state of Georgia, African-American voters were more likely to be required to use outdated and inefficient punch-card machines, which are more likely to invalidate votes, former U.S. Representative Cynthia McKinney testified: "In the majority black precincts of my district, the chaos was so pervasive it could have been planned. . . . There were poorly trained elections workers, old equipment and overcrowded precincts. . . . [Voters had] to stand in line, sometimes outside in the rain and sometimes for as many as five hours. . . ."[11]

Many groups are concerned that, although immigrants who become citizens are legally entitled to vote, barriers such as identification requirements and English-only ballots discourage them from voting. According to the National Council of La Raza, a Latino advocacy organization: "[C]ompared with 62% for Whites and 57% for Blacks, only 45% of Latino voting-age citizens voted in the November 2000 election."[12] The smaller numbers of immigrants and minorities both in the population and in the electorate are reflected in election results. For example, the defeat of Carol Moseley-Braun (D-IL) in the 1998 election left the nation with no African-American or Hispanic senators. In fact, only four African Americans and three Hispanic Americans have ever served in the U.S. Senate.

> • **Currently, bilingual ballots are required only in heavily non-English-speaking communities. Should they be required for any voter who does not speak English well? Should people who do not speak English well be allowed to vote?**

MINORITIES IN THE SENATE

AFRICAN AMERICANS:

Hiram R. Revels (R-Mississippi), 1870–1871

Blanche K. Bruce (R-Mississippi), 1875–1881

Edward W. Brooke (R-Massachusetts), 1967–1979

Carol Moseley-Braun (D-Illinois), 1993–1999

ASIAN AMERICANS:

Hiram L. Fong (R-Hawaii), 1959–1977

Daniel K. Inouye (D-Hawaii), 1963–

Samuel I. Hayakawa (R-California), 1977–1983

Spark M. Matsunaga (D-Hawaii), 1977–1990

Daniel K. Akaka (D-Hawaii), 1990–

HISPANIC AMERICANS:

Octaviano Larrazolo (R-New Mexico), 1928–1929

Dennis Chavez (D-New Mexico), 1935–1962

Joseph M. Montoya (D-New Mexico), 1964–1977

NATIVE AMERICAN INDIAN:

Charles Curtis (R-Kansas), 1907–1913; 1915–1929 (Kaw)

Robert Owen (D-Oklahoma), 1907–1925 (Cherokee)

Ben Nighthorse Campbell (R-Colorado), 1993– (Northern Cheyenne)

From the birth of the nation through 1999, only four African Americans served in the U.S. Senate, along with three Hispanic Americans. This table lists the names of all the minority members who have held seats in the Senate throughout American history.

Current voting rights laws are not enforced strongly enough.

Many civil rights advocates believe that incidents of continued disenfranchisement of the poor, minorities, and immigrants provide proof that our nation's voting rights laws need to be strengthened. As Representative McKinney noted, the Voting Rights Act is subject to abuse by people who obey the letter of the law but violate its spirit. Reflecting on the confusion that occurred in her district during the 2000 election, she charged: "[P]erhaps the [county] leaders . . . don't want large voter participation from the black residents on its south side. That's the only way I can explain the failure to fund adequately the elections office for the past four years. I would argue that this is a subtle violation of the Voting Rights Act with the intent and effect of suppressing the minority vote." [13]

Many civil rights supporters fear that more recent laws, such as the Motor Voter law and the Help America Vote Act, also will be subject to manipulation. Though the Motor Voter law—with its provision that driver's license and welfare offices must actively offer voter registration opportunities—was highly touted as a means of registering large numbers of poor and minority voters, the implementation of the law has been far from perfect.

The U.S. Commission on Civil Rights noted serious flaws in Florida's voter registration process. For example, voters who moved to other counties were issued new driver's licenses, but the department of motor vehicles did not forward their voter registrations to their new counties of residence. Additionally, the department of motor vehicles was unable to account for many voter registrations. The commission's report cited the example of one married couple that had registered to vote when they obtained their driver's licenses. Although the department's records indicated that the couple had indeed registered to vote, the county election office did not have copies of these registrations. The commission concluded: "Mr. and Mrs. Seamans properly registered to vote at their driver license office and were deprived of their right to vote on Election Day." [14]

> • If current laws are not being enforced, is the answer to write new laws?

The Help America Vote Act does not do enough to protect voters' rights.

Although the Help America Vote Act was passed in 2002 as an effort to prevent such mistakes, many people think that the law will not do enough to correct the inequities of the current system. For example, the identification requirements have generated criticism. Senator Charles Schumer (D-NY), who voted against the law, argued that the identification requirements would send the wrong message to voters who have immigrated from countries with oppressive regimes:

> [T]hink of the new immigrant who waited five years and has just become a voter, who doesn't have a car, who is just learning English, and who is afraid of the government where that immigrant came from. You say, You have to do this, this, this, and this. . . .
>
> I have seen the look on the faces of first-time voters who waited in line with their eyes bright with the first chance to exercise their franchise and then were turned away. And they never come back again. [15]

The provisional balloting system seems in theory to guarantee people that their vote will be counted, but many people are not so sure that it will have that effect in practice. The process of verifying the registrations of people casting provisional ballots is subject to the same errors as verifying registrations on site. The National Council of La Raza opposed the legislation, criticizing what it called "an intrusive, error-prone requirement that voters provide a driver's license number or, in the event they do not have one, the last four digits of their Social Security Number." According to the group, this verification process could lead to disenfranchisement: "Election officials must independently verify the number before registering someone, and any individual who has either number but fails to provide it will not be registered."[16] Other groups, such as the American Civil Liberties Union (ACLU), expressed similar concerns.

> • **Is it reasonable to require identification if it intimidates some people? Isn't asking for identification supposed to intimidate people who might otherwise vote fraudulently?**

A major unanswered question surrounding the Help America Vote Act is funding. The law authorized Congress to grant states several billion dollars to improve voting procedures, including replacing outdated punch-card machines; however, the law itself did not appropriate any money to the states. Instead, the law sidestepped the question of funding, leaving Congress to debate the question during its annual budget deliberations. La Raza also criticized the failure to appropriate funding, stating: "[No] one, including the authors of the compromise bill, can guarantee funding sufficient" to replace the outdated voting equipment used predominantly by minority voters.[17]

> • **Why does Congress pass laws but not include funding as part of the law?**

Though prohibited by the U.S. Constitution, there is a long history of voter discrimination against minorities, immigrants, and the poor. Each time the government has passed a law, new types of discrimination have surfaced. Today, civil rights activists believe that discrimination is subtler, but that it still exists. The latest effort to prevent disenfranchisement is the Help America Vote Act of 2002, but many doubt it will do enough to prevent disenfranchisement of minorities, immigrants, and the poor.

Measures Are Needed to Prevent Manipulation of Elections and Voter Fraud

I n spite of anecdotal evidence that eligible voters have been denied the right to vote, not everybody is convinced that stronger voting rights laws are the answer. Many people, especially politically conservative Republicans, feel that voting rights laws go too far. They feel that the fault for people's being turned away from the polls lies not with the system but with the individual voters who did not ensure that they were registered properly. Of greater concern, they believe, is that the generous protections afforded by federal laws actually encourage voter fraud.

Countering arguments that people are too frequently turned away from the polls, critics of generous voting rights laws like to point out how little trouble Mabel and Holly Briscoe had registering to vote in Maryland. Despite claims that older people and people who have just reached voting age are often denied the right to vote, Mabel and Holly had no problems whatsoever registering at the Maryland driver's license office, even though Mabel was in her eighties and Holly was 18.

It took Maryland officials two years to notice anything was wrong with Holly's registration form. Eventually, however, they figured out the problem: Holly was 18 only when her age was measured in *dog years*. State officials discovered the problem when they called Holly for jury duty and Mabel was forced to admit that she had falsified her pet terrier's registration form to prove just how easy the Motor Voter law made voter fraud.

Mabel had not intended for anyone to vote in Holly's name; rather, she registered her dog to vote as a "personal experiment in civic disobedience."[18] She was trying to prove that the Motor Voter law made it too easy for people (not to mention dogs) to vote. Though Maryland officials tried to prosecute her for voter fraud, they ended up dropping the charges in exchange for performance of community service.

Many people, especially conservative Republicans, are convinced that the most important weakness of today's electoral system is not that people are being denied the right to register and vote. They believe that each person has a responsibility to register and vote, and "voting rights" laws merely encourage apathetic voters. Many have accused the Democratic Party of making voting rights an issue not out of fairness but in an effort to increase the number of Democratic voters. The result, they charge, is a system riddled with fraud. Though the Help America Vote Act of 2002 contains anti-fraud provisions, some Republican politicians are concerned that the states will not strictly enforce the provisions.

- **Should the woman who registered her dog have been punished to set an example?**

After the confusing 2000 presidential election, lawmakers took steps to improve the voting process. One part of their effort was the Help America Vote Act, which made a number of changes in election laws. Here, Arkansas politicians watch a slideshow to learn about the changes being brought about by the new law.

Special efforts to register immigrants, minorities, and the poor are politically motivated.

Although supporters of voting rights laws frequently speak of the need to protect the voting rights of immigrants, minorities, and the poor as a matter of civil rights, many conservative Republicans think that the laws represent partisan efforts by Democrats to register voters—such as immigrants, minorities, and the poor—who have traditionally voted Democratic. When the Motor Voter law was passed during the Clinton administration, conservatives widely criticized the law as a thinly veiled effort by the Democratic Party to woo voters who supported the Democrats' social welfare programs. Especially troubling to many critics was the provision requiring that welfare offices provide voter registration forms. The Republican Party favored sweeping welfare reform, making it less likely that welfare recipients would vote Republican.

> • **If you are doing something good (like registering people to vote) but have an ulterior motive (to gain votes), does that make the good act "bad"?**

Many conservatives have suggested that voting rights laws do not remove barriers to voting so much as they try to encourage voting among people who are not willing to make any special efforts in order to register to vote. Jonah Goldberg, editor of *National Review Online*, wrote: "Motor-voter supporters, and others who bemoan low turnout, have never satisfactorily addressed a fundamental question: Why should we care that people who don't care enough to vote aren't voting?"[19] In their opinion, voting is a privilege as well as a right, and therefore people can be expected to make special efforts to register and vote. Conservatives have poked fun at efforts such as "Rock the Vote," in which popular musicians encourage young people to register and vote.

One example of a voter-registration drive that has drawn heavy criticism was the effort to register Native American voters during the 2002 senatorial election in South Dakota. The combined efforts of the state and national Democratic parties led to the registration of 17,000 new voters in the sparsely

THE LETTER OF THE LAW

The "Motor Voter" Law's Registration Requirements

[E]ach State shall establish procedures to register to vote in elections for Federal office ...

(1) Each State motor vehicle driver's license application (including any renewal application) submitted to the appropriate State motor vehicle authority under State law shall serve as an application for voter registration with respect to elections for Federal office unless the applicant fails to sign the voter registration application.

(2) An application for voter registration submitted under paragraph (1) shall be considered as updating any previous voter registration by the applicant....

(1) Each State shall designate agencies for the registration of voters in elections for Federal office.

(2) Each State shall designate as voter registration agencies —
   (A) all offices in the State that provide public assistance; and
   (B) all offices in the State that provide State-funded programs primarily engaged in providing services to persons with disabilities.

(3)(A) In addition to voter registration agencies designated under paragraph (2), each State shall designate other offices within the State as voter registration agencies.
   (B) Voter registration agencies designated under subparagraph (A) may include —
      (i) State or local government offices such as public libraries, public schools, offices of city and county clerks (including marriage license bureaus), fishing and hunting license bureaus, government revenue offices, unemployment compensation offices, and offices not described in paragraph (2)(B) that provide services to persons with disabilities; and
      (ii) Federal and nongovernmental offices, with the agreement of such offices.

Source: National Voter Registration Act, 42 U.S.C. §§ 1973gg-2-1973gg-5.

populated state. Although it was true that, prior to the registration campaign, many Native Americans living on the state's nine
reservations had either not registered to vote or had registered
but not voted regularly, some criticized the Democratic Party's
voter-registration efforts as being designed to win votes rather
than to encourage civic participation. Ultimately, in the
statewide senatorial election, the Democratic candidate, Tim
Johnson, beat his Republican challenger by 524 votes.

> • **Should Republicans criticize Democrats for registering
> voters improperly, or should they conduct their own voter
> registration drives?**

In an article for the conservative *National Review* magazine,
Byron York criticized the Democrats' tactics for registering
voters, calling their practice of paying "bounty hunters" three
dollars for each person whom they registered to vote an
"invitation to fraud."[20] He also questioned Democrats' Election
Day activities, including renting vans and hiring drivers to bring
people to the polls. Republican poll volunteer Ed Assman told
York that Democratic poll workers were giving cash to the van
drivers. "I heard the driver say, 'We need money.' . . . The guy
rolled out cash and gave cash to each guy," Assman said.[21]
Although the Democrats explained that this was "gas money,"
and the state's attorney general found no credible evidence of
Democrats paying people to vote, the news of drivers being
given cash raised many Republicans' suspicions.

In efforts to register immigrants, who traditionally have
voted overwhelmingly Democratic, some conservative
Republicans have suggested that Democrats have even targeted
non-citizens. Jim Boulet, Jr., executive director of English
First (an organization supporting the adoption of English as
the United States' official language), criticized the Democratic
Party for sending a letter, in English and Spanish, to people
not registered to vote, encouraging them to register. The
letter reached at least one non-citizen and probably many

others. Boulet also asserted that during the Democratic administration of Bill Clinton, immigration laws were bent or broken in an effort to register more immigrant voters. He writes: "Al Gore helped Bill Clinton trade permanent U.S. citizenship for Democratic votes in 1996 and beyond," charging the former vice president with turning Citizenship USA, a program designed to help immigrants become citizens "into 'a pro-Democrat voter mill' in which English tests were waived and criminal records of prospective citizens swept under the rug."[22]

> • Should political parties be blamed for fraudulent votes, or does the blame lie with local governments for not screening out fraudulent votes?

In the same way that many conservatives criticize voting rights laws as the Democratic Party's effort to increase the number of registered Democrats, many critics also charge that claims of disenfranchisement are not genuinely motivated by concern that voters have their voices heard, but are really partisan efforts by the Democrats to increase their votes. Although the U.S. Commission on Civil Rights concluded that there was widespread voter disenfranchisement in Florida during the 2000 presidential election, many have disputed that claim, believing instead that efforts to discredit the Florida election constituted a partisan effort by Democrats to weaken public confidence in President Bush.

Two members of the commission filed a dissenting report criticizing the commission's findings. Commissioners Abigail Thernstrom and Russell G. Redenbaugh wrote that the number of disqualified ballots was not evidence of disenfranchisement: "Disenfranchisement is not the same thing as voter error. [Many of the disqualified ballots] are due to voter error. Or machine error, which is random, and thus cannot 'disenfranchise' any population group."[23]

The dissenting commissioners wrote that, in addition to

being unsupported by the facts, accusations of disenfranchisement were being levied at the wrong people. Although much of the criticism focused on Republican Governor Jeb Bush and Republican Secretary of State Katherine Harris, the supervision of elections was in the hands of county-level election supervisors. The commissioners noted: "[O]f the 25 counties with the highest spoilage rates, the election was supervised by a Democrat—the one exception being an official with no party affiliation."[24] In other words, local Democratic politicians had botched the election, but after Republican George W. Bush won the presidential race, Democrats used charges of racism to criticize the Florida's Republican administration and call the election into doubt.

> • **Should state governments or the federal government take control of federal elections from local officials?**

So-called "voting rights" laws have caused widespread fraud.

The story of Mabel Briscoe, who registered her dog to vote in Maryland, attracted national headlines, mostly as a humorous anecdote. The terrier never voted, and so no harm was done, many people thought. However, like the Maryland officials who wanted to prosecute the 82-year-old woman, some people did not think the story was funny at all. Rather, the story was a reminder that many people not only register their dogs to vote, but take advantage of the registrations to vote illegally.

Senator Christopher Bond (R-MO) alleged that illegal voting was rampant in Missouri—including at least one case of a *dead dog* that had supposedly cast a ballot. According to Bond: "3,000 ballots [were] dropped off before the mayoral primary in St. Louis in 2001. . . . [M]ost of those 3,000 were in the same handwriting and were for new registrants on one or two city blocks."[25]

John Samples, the director of the Center for Representative Government at the Cato Institute, attributed the widespread voting fraud to efforts by political parties to register minority voters. Referring to the same St. Louis mayoral election criticized by Bond, Samples testified to a Senate committee:

> [A] national campaign—promoted by Democrats—to register more African-American voters and get them to the polling booth . . . delivered 3,800 voter registration cards . . . [on] the deadline for the March mayoral primary. . . .
>
> [N]early all of them were fraudulent. Many of them sought to register prominent people, dead or alive—as well as at least three deceased aldermen and a dog. . . . They also found cards for convicted felons and for residents who did not seek to register themselves in the primary.[26]

However, Samples testified, such problems were by no means limited to Missouri. Samples identified other states in which the Motor Voter act had led to voter fraud:

> In Indiana . . . tens of thousands of people appear on the voter rolls more than once . . . more than 300 dead people were registered, and . . . three convicted killers and two convicted child molesters were on the rolls. In general, experts believe one in five names on the rolls in Indiana do not belong there. A recent study in Georgia found more than 15,000 dead people on active voting rolls statewide. Alaska, according to Federal Election Commission, had 502,968 names on its voter rolls in 1998. The census estimates only 437,000 people of voting age were living in the state that year.[27]

Samples asserted that the Motor Voter act had made it impossible for the states to control voter fraud. At the same time that the Motor Voter law made it much easier for people to submit fraudulent registrations, it also made it much more difficult for states to remove people from the list of registered voters:

[To] remove a voter who has moved from the rolls of a voting district, the local jurisdiction has two choices. First, they could get written confirmation of the move from the citizen. Lacking that, the jurisdiction had to send a notice to the voter. If the notice card was not returned and the person did not vote in two general elections for Federal office after the notice was sent, then the jurisdiction could remove their name from the rolls.[28]

> • **Is there a way to make it easier to vote without allowing fraud? What about requiring Social Security numbers?**

THE LETTER OF THE LAW

The "Motor Voter" Law's List of Maintenance Requirements

(d) Removal of names from voting rolls

(1) A State shall not remove the name of a registrant from the official list of eligible voters in elections for Federal office on the ground that the registrant has changed residence unless the registrant—

(A) confirms in writing that the registrant has changed residence to a place outside the registrar's jurisdiction in which the registrant is registered; or

(B) (i) has failed to respond to a notice described in paragraph (2); and

(ii) has not voted or appeared to vote (and, if necessary, correct the registrar's record of the registrant's address) in an election during the period beginning on the date of the notice and ending on the day after the date of the second general election for Federal office that occurs after the date of the notice.

(2) A notice is described in this paragraph if it is a postage prepaid and pre-addressed return card, sent by forwardable mail, on which the registrant may state his or her current address. . . .

Source: National Voter Registration Act, 42 U.S.C. § 1973g

Strict enforcement of the Help America Vote Act is necessary to prevent future fraud.

While Congress deliberated the Help America Vote Act, much of the controversy centered on the law's anti-fraud provisions, with the split following strict party lines. The reason Congress took nearly two years to respond to the widespread problems of the 2000 election with this law streamlining registration and voting procedures was that Democrats viewed strict anti-fraud provisions as a means of disenfranchising voters. Republicans, on the other hand, thought that any law making it easier for eligible citizens to register and vote must simultaneously make it more difficult for dishonest people to register and vote fraudulently.

During Senate debates, Senator Bond expressed frustration with Democratic opposition to provisions requiring that first-time voters who register by mail provide a form of identification in order to vote: "[We] devised a compromise that . . . did not impose any unreasonable restrictions on voters who might not have a driver's license, for example. That is why we said voters can use a bank statement, a government check, utility bill, anything that has your name and address on it. . . ."[29]

Unable to defeat the law's identification requirements, Democrats waged a battle in the press after passage of the law, arguing that states could make up their own mind about allowing people to register. Senator Christopher Dodd (D-CT) told *The New York Times*, "The legislation does not establish federal registration eligibility requirements. . . . Nothing in this legislation prohibits a state from registering an applicant once the verification process takes place," which, according to the article, includes cases in which "a would-be voter provides inaccurate or incomplete information."[30]

Senator Bond challenged his colleague's interpretation of the law, saying, "It is the intent of Congress to impose a new federal mandate for voter registration."[31] Democrats and civil

Voter Registration Application
For U.S. Citizens

You can use this form to: ■ register to vote ■ report that your name or address has changed ■ register with a party	This space for office use only.

Please print in blue or black ink

1 — Mr. Mrs. Miss Ms. | Last Name | First Name | Middle Name(s) | (Circle one) Jr Sr II III IV

2 — Address (see instructions)— Street (or route and box number) | Apt. or Lot # | City/Town | State | Zip Code

3 — Address Where You Get Your Mail If Different From Above (see instructions) | City/Town | State | Zip Code

4 — Date of Birth / / Month Day Year | **5** Telephone Number (optional) | **6** ID Number (see item 6 in the instructions for your State)

7 — Choice of Party (see item 7 in the instructions for your State) | **8** Race or Ethnic Group (see item 8 in the instructions for your State)

9 — I swear/affirm that:
- I am a United States citizen
- I meet the eligibility requirements of my state and subscribe to any oath required.

(See item 9 in the instructions for your state before you sign.)

- The information I have provided is true to the best of my knowledge under penalty of perjury. If I have provided false information, I may be fined, imprisoned, or (if not a U.S. citizen) deported from or refused entry to the United States.

Please sign full name (or put mark) ↓

Date: / / Month Day Year

10 — If the applicant is unable to sign, who helped the applicant fill out this application? Give name, address and phone number (phone number optional).

Fold here

Please fill out the sections below if they apply to you.

If this application is for a change of name, what was your name before you changed it?

A — Mr. Mrs. Miss Ms. | Last Name | First Name | Middle Name(s) | (Circle one) Jr Sr II III IV

If you were registered before but this is the first time you are registering from the address in Box 2, what was your address where you were registered before?

B — Street (or route and box number) | Apt. or Lot # | City/Town | State | Zip Code

If you live in a rural area but do not have a street number, or if you have no address, please show on the map where you live.

C —
- Write in the names of the crossroads (or streets) nearest to where you live.
- Draw an X to show where you live.
- Use a dot to show any schools, churches, stores, or other landmarks near where you live, and write the name of the landmark.

NORTH ↑

Example: Route #2 | ● Grocery Store | Woodchuck Road | Public School ● | X

To Mail:
1. Address the back of this application (see address under your state).
2. Remove plastic strip below.
3. Fold form at middle and seal at top.
4. Put on a first-class stamp and mail.

Revised 7/12/2002

Some critics argue that widespread efforts to recruit minority and immigrant voters have led to increased voting fraud. By giving untruthful answers to certain questions on the voter registration application (seen here), a person might register to vote illegally fairly easily.

FOR OFFICIAL USE ONLY

FIRST CLASS
STAMP
NECESSARY
FOR
MAILING

OFFICIAL
ELECTION MAIL
Authorized by the U.S. Postal Service

Revised 7/12/2002

rights organizations might pressure states to continue processing inaccurate or incomplete applications—for example, applications in which the registrant fails to answer the question, "Are you a citizen of the United States of America?" Senator Dodd has suggested that the legislation requires the states to ask the question but does not require them to invalidate applications in which the answer is left blank. Republicans, including Senator Bond, however, believe that, unless states follow the spirit of the law and only register voters who provide complete and accurate information, rampant voter fraud will continue.

> • **If a state's government disagrees with a federal law, what should the state government do?**

Many political conservatives believe that the biggest problem facing American elections is not that people are being denied the right to vote, but that too many people are voting fraudulently. They support stricter registration and identification requirements and question massive voter registration drives, saying that each person should take the responsibility to register and vote. Many Republicans, believing that many "voting rights" measures are disguised efforts to gain Democratic votes, want to see voting fraud measures strictly enforced.

Money Is Corrupting American Democracy

Running successfully for political office in the United States requires an incredible amount of money. According to Kathleen Murphy, who covers election issues for *Stateline.org*, the *losing* candidates in 2002 governors' races in California and Texas spent over $50 million and close to $70 million, respectively, while "[c]andidates for governor in New York could have bought every voter two Big Macs with fries and Cokes for about half the amount they spent on the race."[32] Considering that nearly 20 million people live in the state, that's a lot of hamburgers!

> • Soft drink companies spend millions of dollars to promote their products. Why should political candidates not do the same?

Most of the money for campaigns has come from contributions from individuals, corporations, or special interest groups.

ELECTION STATS 2000

SENATE*

Average Winner Spent	$7,266,576
Average Loser Spent	$3,864,638
Most Expensive Campaign	$63,209,506
Most Expensive Campaigner	Jon S. Corzine (D-NJ)
Least Expensive Winning Campaign	$630,965
Least Expensive Winning Campaigner	Daniel K. Akaka (D-HI)
Number of Incumbents Seeking Re-election	29
Number of Incumbents Reelected	23
Incumbents Re-election Rate	79%
Number of Close Races (winning margin less than 10%)	10
Average Winner's Vote Percentage	60%
Average Winner's Receipts from Political Action Committees (PACs)	$1,086,982
Most Receipts from PACs	$2,978,161
Candidate with Most PAC Receipts	Spencer Abraham (R-MI)
Average Winner's End-of-year Campaign Balance	$642,801
Biggest End-of-year Campaign Balance	$4,622,229
Candidate with Largest End-of-year Campaign Balance	Kay Bailey Hutchison (R-TX)

HOUSE

Average Winner Spent	$840,300
Average Loser Spent	$307,121
Most Expensive Campaign	$6,964,933
Most Expensive Campaigner	James F. Humphreys (D-WV)
Least Expensive Winning Campaign	$56,828
Least Expensive Winning Campaigner	Norman Sisisky (D-VA)
Number of Incumbents Seeking Re-election	403
Number of Incumbents Reelected	394
Incumbents Re-election Rate	98%
Number of Close Races (winning margin less than 10%)	42
Average Winner's Vote Percentage	69%
Average Winner's Receipts from PACs	$381,891
Most Receipts from PACs	$1,316,733
Candidate with Most PAC Receipts	E. Clay Shaw Jr. (R-FL)
Average Winner's End-of-year Campaign Balance	$272,817
Biggest End-of-year Campaign Balance	$2,360,082
Candidate with Largest End-of-year Campaign Balance	Peter Deutsch (D-FL)

* Figures cover full six-year cycle for Senate incumbents

Averages include all incumbent politicians and major party challengers in the general election. Third-party challengers are not included, as their number and relative lack of funds tend to artificially lower the averages.

Loser averages are based on the money raised and spent by the candidate who came in second on Election Day. Where candidates ran unopposed, losers' spending and fundraising are counted as $0.

The amount of money spent on political campaigns has skyrocketed in recent years. As this table demonstrates, in the 2000 elections, the average winner of a Senate race spent well over $7 million, while a newly elected member of the House of Representatives spent over $800,000.

Some politicians are concerned that the amount of money being pumped into political campaigns has created a corrupt government in which elected officials care more about contributors than they do about the people who elect them. Champions of "campaign finance reform" such as Senators John McCain and Russ Feingold believe that limits on fundraising activities are needed to preserve the integrity of American democracy. Although McCain and Feingold won passage of a federal law, the Bipartisan Campaign Reform Act of 2002 (BCRA), numerous individuals and organizations have challenged the law in court. It is therefore likely that the campaign finance debate will continue in the courts and in Congress for years to come. Similar debates are taking place at the state level; some states have campaign finance laws and others do not.

Some of the most controversial provisions of federal election laws deal with campaign contributions, including:

- Limits on individual campaign contributions
  to $2,000 (raised by the BCRA—the Bipartisan
  Campaign Reform Act of 2002—from the previous
  limit of $1,000).[33]

THE LETTER OF THE LAW

Bipartisan Campaign Reform Act Subjects "Soft Money" to Same Limits as Other Contributions

SOFT MONEY OF POLITICAL PARTIES.
  (a) NATIONAL COMMITTEES.—
    (1) IN GENERAL.—A national committee of a political party (including a national congressional campaign committee of a political party) may not solicit, receive, or direct to another person a contribution, donation, or transfer of funds or any other thing of value, or spend any funds, that are not subject to the limitations, prohibitions, and reporting requirements of this Act.

- Prohibition of most campaign contributions by corporations and labor unions (extended by the BCRA to ban contributions to political parties).[34]

FROM THE BENCH

Campaign Contributions Receive Lessened Protection Under First Amendment

[A] limitation upon the amount that any one person or group may contribute to a candidate or political committee entails only a marginal restriction upon the contributor's ability to engage in free communication. A contribution serves as a general expression of support for the candidate and his views, but does not communicate the underlying basis for the support. The quantity of communication by the contributor does not increase perceptibly with the size of his contribution, since the expression rests solely on the undifferentiated, symbolic act of contributing. At most, the size of the contribution provides a very rough index of the intensity of the contributor's support for the candidate. A limitation on the amount of money a person may give to a candidate or campaign organization thus involves little direct restraint on his political communication, for it permits the symbolic expression of support evidenced by a contribution but does not in any way infringe the contributor's freedom to discuss candidates and issues. While contributions may result in political expression if spent by a candidate or an association to present views to the voters, the transformation of contributions into political debate involves speech by someone other than the contributor.

Given the important role of contributions in financing political campaigns, contribution restrictions could have a severe impact on political dialogue if the limitations prevented candidates and political committees from amassing the resources necessary for effective advocacy. There is no indication, however, that the contribution limitations imposed by the Act would have any dramatic adverse effect on the funding of campaigns and political associations. The overall effect of the Act's contribution ceilings is merely to require candidates and political committees to raise funds from a greater number of persons and to compel people who would otherwise contribute amounts greater than the statutory limits to expend such funds on direct political expression, rather than to reduce the total amount of money potentially available to promote political expression.

Source: *Buckley* v. *Valeo*, 424 U.S. 1 (1976) (per curiam).

Prior to passage of the BCRA, federal election law was largely the result of decisions by the Federal Election Commission (a federal agency) and the landmark 1976 Supreme Court decision in *Buckley* v. *Valeo*. In that case, the Court upheld limits on contributions to candidates; however, the Court noted that the First Amendment's guarantee of free speech invalidated many other aspects of federal election law.

Although federal law limited their ability to contribute money directly to candidates, many corporations, labor unions, and wealthy individuals still wanted to be able to influence the political process. As a result, they began to make large contributions to the Democratic and Republican parties. Although the contributions allowed the parties to campaign for candidates, the contributions did not technically violate the law, earning them the nickname "soft money." Senator Feingold wrote that soft money transforms "our representative democracy" into a "corporate democracy, in which the 'one person, one vote' principle is supplanted by a system that allocates influence over the political process in proportion to the amount of money an individual or group puts into that process."[35]

Although the BCRA banned soft money, there have been numerous court challenges to the law, and campaign finance reformers have found themselves having to continue defending the ban on soft money. Reformers firmly believe that soft money has a corrupting influence on Congress and has caused the public to lose faith in the political process. They reject the idea that campaign contributions are a form of "free speech" protected by the First Amendment, believing that, if anything, political contributions take power away from individual voters and concentrate it in the hands of the wealthy.

- **Were soft money donors taking advantage of a loophole or taking advantage of their freedom of speech?**

	To any candidate or candidate committee (per election*)	To any national party committee (per year)	To any PAC, state/ local party, or other political committee (per year)	Aggregate total
Individual can give**:	Old law: $1,000	$20,000	$5,000	$25,000 per year
	New law: $2,000, subject to the aggregate limit***	$25,000 per party committee, subject to the aggregate limit	• $10,000 to each state or local party committee • $5,000 to each PAC or other political committee, subject to the aggregate limit	$95,000 per two-year election cycle as follows: •$37,500 per cycle to candidates; and •$57,500 per cycle to all national party committees and PACs ($20,000 to $57,500 per cycle to all national party committees, and a maximum $37,500 per cycle to PACs)
Multicandidate committee can give****:	Old law: $5,000	$15,000	$5,000	No Limit
	New law: Same	Same	Same	Same
Other political committee can give:	Old law: $1,000	$20,000	$5,000	No Limit
	New law: Same	Same	Same	Same

* Primary and general elections count as separate elections.

** Individual contribution limits under the new law will be indexed for inflation.

*** Individual contribution limits under the new law are higher to candidates facing wealthy opponents financing their own election.

**** Multicandidate committees are those with more than 50 contributors, that have been registered for at least six months, and (with the exception of state party committees) have made contributions to five or more federal candidates.

Under the Bipartisan Campaign Reform Act (BCRA), candidates for political office are restricted in the amount of money they can accept for their campaigns, and may not accept money from certain sources. This chart shows some of the changes mandated by the 2002 law.

Soft money obligates elected officials to corporate interests rather than the public interest.

The movement for campaign finance reform gained momentum as a growing number of people began to believe that many members of Congress no longer represented the interests of the people who elected them. Instead, it was feared, members of Congress primarily represented the interests of the corporations and other interest groups making the soft money donations that allowed them to campaign successfully.

Supporters of campaign finance reform do not necessarily accuse members of Congress and other politicians of allowing their votes to be bought; however, the line between accepting a bribe and being overly influenced by campaign contributions can be somewhat murky. As an illustration, environmental laws can have an enormous impact on the profitability of chemical manufacturers. If, while Congress was debating new pollution laws, a chemical company trying to influence a particular senator's vote gave him or her $50,000 to buy a new car, this payment would constitute bribery, a serious crime. Yet, if the same chemical company gave $50,000 to the senator's political party to help with a re-election campaign, this type of "soft money" contribution would have been perfectly legal prior to passage of the BCRA—or if the courts strike down the law.

> • **Does the distinction between bribery and campaign contributions make sense? Isn't it money either way?**

Although the soft money contribution in this illustration would not have obliged the senator to support the chemical company's position, the desire for future financial support would be likely to have a tremendous influence on his or her vote. Supporters of campaign finance reform view this influence as a problem in itself. Senator Christopher Dodd has argued: "Money . . . threatens to drown out the voice of the average voter of average means; money . . . creates the appearance that a wealthy few have a disproportionate say over public policy; and money . . . places extensive demands on the time of candidates—time that they and the voters believe is better spent discussing and debating the issues of the day." [36]

Surprisingly, despite the possibility of gaining political influence through soft money contributions, not all business leaders opposed the BCRA's soft money ban. Denouncing what it called the "perversion of the soft money system into a widely acknowledged 'pay to play' scheme by both major parties," [37] the Committee for Economic Development, a group of business leaders and educators, argued that the soft money system placed unfair pressures on businesses: "Because the stakes are so high for solicited businesses, the reality is that soft money payments . . . are commonly made out of fear of the consequences of refusing to give or refusing to give enough." [38]

In the committee's view, soft money has a cause-and-effect relationship with legislation:

> It is not surprising that the largest soft money contributors tend to be companies in industries that are heavily regulated by the federal government or those whose profits can be dramatically affected by government policy. These donors are solicited by Members of Congress who sit on committees that consider matters directly affecting the financial health or operation of the companies being solicited. [39]

> • **Is it unethical for an elected official to ask for contributions from companies that can gain or lose based on what the official does?**

The effect of corporate campaign spending has not escaped public notice. Companies such as Enron, the energy company that made headlines because of widespread accounting irregularities, and Philip Morris, which profited from selling hazardous tobacco products, were significant soft money donors. These companies curried favor in Congress while members of the public lost their retirement savings because of the drop in Enron's stock price and suffered and died from the harmful effects of smoking. The influence of such corporations with elected officials has eroded the public's confidence in American democracy.

Arguing in support of the BCRA in a 2001 Senate debate, Senator McCain said: "[According to] a poll that *Time* magazine has conducted over many years . . . [in] 1961, 76% of Americans said yes to the question, 'Do you trust your government to do the right thing?' This year, only 19% of Americans still believe that."[40] According to the Committee for Economic Development, "Fully two-thirds of the public think that their own representative in Congress would listen to the views of outsiders who made large political contributions before a constituent's views."[41]

> • **Do you trust your government to do the right thing? Does your answer have anything to do with campaign contributions?**

Unlimited individual campaign contributions defeat the principle of "one person, one vote."

Campaign finance reformers are concerned not only with corporate "soft money" donations but also with the effect of individual contributions by wealthy donors. Part of the compromise that led to the passage of the BCRA was increasing the limit that an individual can contribute to a candidate in a federal election from $1,000 to $2,000, but at the same time extending the restrictions to individual contributions to political parties. However, opponents of campaign finance restrictions continue to question whether there should be any limits on the amount of money a person can give to a candidate (or political party) of his or her choice. There have been a number of court challenges to the individual donation limits for federal elections, and many have challenged state contribution limits, both in court and in the state legislatures.

"OH GREAT! CHECKOUT TIME WAS 11:00AM AND IT'S ALMOST NOON—NOW HE'S GOING TO CHARGE US ANOTHER $100,000."

One of the most prevalent problems in political campaigning is the granting of favors to potential contributors in order to win support. This political cartoon pokes fun at one recent example of this.

Like corporate soft money, individual contributions to political parties received a great deal of negative attention during the 1996 elections. Opponents of President Bill Clinton charged him with selling access to the White House in exchange for contributions to the Democratic Party. People who attended White House coffees had frequently contributed tens of thousands of dollars. But scandal really broke out when the press revealed that several people, each of whom had contributed hundreds of thousands to the Democratic National Committee, were invited to sleep in the historic Lincoln Bedroom at the White House.

Although critics charged that Clinton was abusing both his elected office and the sanctity of the White House itself, the Clinton administration denied that it was running a hotel service for wealthy contributors and maintained that no laws were broken. The scandal was repeated in 2000 when Clinton, already on his way out of the White House, opened the Lincoln Bedroom to people who had donated money to Democratic causes while his wife, Hillary, was running for the Senate. Scandals such as this helped to gain support for the BCRA's limits on individual donations to political parties.

> • **Is there a difference between elected officials asking for money and challengers asking for money? Is it fair that the president can "rent out" the White House but challengers cannot?**

Another controversial issue is regulating who could donate money to candidates and who could not. During early deliberations about the BCRA, some suggested restricting the amount of money that a candidate for the Senate or House of Representatives could raise from out of state. While only residents of Georgia, for example, may vote for that state's senators and representatives, federal law does not prohibit residents of other states from contributing money to candidates in Georgia's congressional elections.

Events during the 2002 congressional elections demonstrated that out-of-state money plays a large role in determining the outcome of elections. During primary elections in Alabama and Georgia, incumbent Representatives Earl Hilliard and Cynthia McKinney lost their parties' nominations (and therefore their seats) to challengers who benefited greatly from out-of-state money. In both cases, the incumbent and the victor were each African American; in both cases, a majority of the voters in the district were African American. However, both campaigns attracted significant donations from people who were neither African American nor residents of the Deep South. According to the *Montgomery Advertiser*, Hilliard's challenger, Artur Davis, raised just over $306,000 in individual contributions, and nearly $189,000 of these contributions came from New York. McKinney's challenger,

Denise Majette, also raised a significant amount of out-of-state money.[42]

The reason that the races attracted so much money from out of state was that Hilliard and McKinney had both taken anti-Israel positions, angering many Jewish people across the nation. Journalist Jonathan Rosenblum extolled, "Jewish political activists scored impressive victories in two recent Congressional primaries," noting that a majority of the funding for Hilliard and McKinney's challengers had come from "out-of-state Jewish contributors."[43] Many applauded the defeats, pleased that an organized effort had removed two anti-Israel votes from the House of Representatives.

However, not everyone agreed that this was a case of democracy working properly. Many people were concerned that the outcome of races between two African Americans in African-American districts would be so heavily influenced by non-African-American contributors, according to the leader of the Congressional Black Caucus, Representative Eddie Bernice Johnson (D-TX). She expressed concern that many African Americans feel as though "Jewish people are attempting to pick our leaders."[44]

A broader concern is that interest groups can selectively "buy" seats in Congress by targeting elections in which the candidates would otherwise not be able to raise significant campaign funds—for example in less affluent congressional districts, or less affluent or less populous states. This raises the question of whether an official so elected would represent his or her constituents or the people who paid for his or her campaign. Would Davis and Majette be willing to take a position that would be popular with African-American voters in the Deep South but unpopular with potential Jewish contributors in New York?

- **Would the Alabama and Georgia elections have been controversial if race were not a factor? Should race play a role in choosing a candidate?**

Campaign contributions are not "free speech" deserving of full First Amendment protection.

Recently, many people opposed to campaign finance reform have attacked the Supreme Court's ruling in *Buckley* v. *Valeo* that political contributions receive a lesser level of protection under the First Amendment than either political speech or expenditures on advertising about political issues. However, reformers support the holding in *Buckley*, maintaining that there is an important distinction between political speech and the infusion of money into politics.

The First Amendment to the U.S. Constitution states, "Congress shall make no law . . . abridging the freedom of speech. . . ." However, campaign finance reformers such as Senator Christopher Dodd believe that Congress *can* regulate campaign contributions:

> [P]olitical speech should be unlimited. . . . But to equate speech with money is not only a false equation, it is also a dangerous one to our democracy.
>
> When that speech and those ideas are paid for overwhelmingly by a few wealthy individuals or groups or foreign nationals or anonymous groups or by undisclosed contributors, the speech is neither free nor democratic. It is encumbered by unknown special interests who have paid for it. And it minimizes or excludes the speech of those who lack substantial resources to counter it.[45]

In support of the BCRA's provisions limiting soft money contributions, a coalition of former leaders of the ACLU argued:

> The First Amendment is designed to promote a functioning and fair democracy. The current system of campaign financing makes a mockery of that ideal by enabling wealthy and powerful interests effectively to set the national agenda. . . . [W]hen the government intervenes to restore

the integrity of the democratic process, it enhances, rather than retards, First Amendment interests.[46]

Although the ACLU itself opposed the BCRA, the fact that former leaders of the ACLU took a position arguing for a narrow interpretation of the First Amendment is particularly remarkable. Throughout the years, the ACLU has argued that the First Amendment's protections are almost boundless, and that pornography, flag burning, and KKK marches are all protected forms of expression.

- **Should wealthy people have a right to "more" free speech than poor people?**

The Bipartisan Campaign Reform Act of 2002 was a response to widespread concerns that money is corrupting American democracy. Corporations, special interest groups, and wealthy individuals have pumped millions of dollars into election campaigns, causing many to wonder whether politicians represent the interest of the voters or the big-time contributors. With numerous court challenges to the BCRA and debates continuing at the state level, the debate over campaign finance reform will continue for years to come.

Campaign Contributions Are a Vital Part of the Democratic Process

A lthough political polls indicate that Americans have lost faith in their elected officials, and although the Bipartisan Campaign Reform Act (BCRA) passed with the support of both major parties, not everyone supports campaign finance "reform." In fact, many people believe that campaign finance restrictions actually harm the democratic process.

Many politicians and members of the press act as though it is a foregone conclusion that there is too much money in politics. Recall the article comparing the cost of the New York governor's race to burgers and fries. However, others use the same analogy to claim that there is actually not enough money spent on campaigning. In 2000, journalist Tom Bethell wrote: "In the latest election cycle, $675 million was spent contesting House and Senate seats. With 196 million eligible votes, this is less than $4 a head, or, as Sen. [Mitch] McConnell [R.-KY] likes to say, less than the price of a McDonald's extra value meal."[47] In the senator's opinion, the cost of a fast-food meal is not enough for educating voters about campaign issues.

When compared with the overall amount of money that Congress spends each year, the amount of money spent on political campaigns seems even less significant. As Bethell points out, in 1998 Senate races, winning candidates spent an average of just under $5 million. To Bethell, this seems like a wise investment: "Congress spends about $1.7 trillion a year, and a senator will be in office for six years. Thus $5 million 'buys' a one-hundredth share of control over the disposition of about ten trillion dollars."[48] Taking the math a step further, each dollar spent on the campaign enables the senator to control one percent of $2 million in spending.

People like Bethell are not seriously suggesting that a political campaign is a financial investment like purchasing stocks and bonds. Many supporters of soft money feel that banning soft money ignores the real problem of American politics—that the federal government spends far too much money and regulates businesses too strictly. In the words of the Cato Institute's Doug Bandow: "As long as Uncle Sam hands out nearly $2 trillion in loot every year and uses its rule-making power to enrich or impoverish entire industries, individuals and companies will spend millions to influence the process."[49]

Opponents of campaign finance restrictions opposed the BCRA in Congress, and continue to challenge the law in the courts. They believe that the system of soft money actually aids democracy by helping to maintain political parties, and that individual contributions allow people to participate fully in government. They back up their concerns with constitutional arguments that limits on campaign contributions violate the First Amendment by restricting freedom of speech.

> • Does the high price of running a campaign limit the voters'
>   choice of candidates? Do all politicians seem pretty much the
>   same to you?

Contributions to political parties are an essential part of the political process.

Opponents of campaign finance restrictions believe that so-called "soft money" contributions are an important part of the political process, chiefly because they benefit the American political party system. For the past two centuries, each president of the United States has been elected with the backing of a major political party, and since the Civil War, the Democratic and Republican parties have dominated national politics.

Many people believe that voter apathy and declining confidence in the political system can be traced to a decline in the major parties—a decline that will become worse if the ban on soft money contributions to political parties is enforced. Political science professor Steven E. Schier believes that experience in the United States and elsewhere demonstrates that political parties are necessary for democracy to thrive. He writes: "Throughout American history, political parties have performed vital services for our democracy. . . . Most of the world's democracies that have survived 25 years or more have had stable party systems with a low number of parties."[50] Supporters of the party system have developed a number of theories as to how the party system supports democracy.

> • **Does it make sense that the Democratic and Republican parties have dominated politics for so long? Do you identify strongly with either party?**

One reason that political parties aid democracy is that they unite members of society behind political issues. A citizen who supports and trusts a particular political party does not have to study complicated matters such as environmental regulations and health-care programs—not to mention election law—or carefully analyze each candidate's position on every issue. Political parties make voting much simpler, writes

Schier, "encouraging those with less education and less income to vote. . . . Choosing between two teams rather than among a plethora of individual candidates makes it easier for more citizens to cast an informed vote."[51]

> • **Can people trust political parties to take the right stands on important issues?**

Political parties have played a major role in registering voters and getting them to the polls. In fact, the soft money system originally developed as a way for interest groups, corporations, and unions to financially support what Senator Feingold has called "party-building activities such as get-out-the-vote campaigns and voter registration drives."[52] Many people agree that such efforts are necessary to encourage more people to vote; however, it will be more difficult for parties to conduct these activities if the soft money ban is enforced. Attorney Allison R. Hayward writes, "[S]pecial-interest groups, corporations, and unions . . . could also engage in voter-registration activities once pursued by parties, but one should doubt that interest groups would pursue these activities on the same scale as parties."[53] Sponsoring these activities individually would not be as efficient as allowing these organizations to contribute soft money to the parties to do them.

Another benefit of the party system that is hampered by the soft money ban is that political parties play a major role in helping new candidates challenge incumbent politicians. In many states, a single party dominates politics, which makes fundraising difficult because people do not want to contribute to what they see as a losing cause. In other states, politicians have represented their constituencies for decades and challengers have difficulties overcoming the incumbent's name recognition. In such states, voters often feel as though they have no choice in selecting their government officials. In South Carolina, for example, Strom Thurmond held onto his Senate seat until retiring in January 2003 at age 100. Although many people opposed Thurmond, who had run for president in 1948 under the slogan "Segregation Forever," the opposition was never strong enough to unseat him.

> • Why do you think that it is so hard for challengers to defeat elected officials who have been in office for many years?

With access to soft money, national political parties were able to help their candidate's campaign, even if there was strong local opposition. John Samples of the Cato Institute writes, "America needs more competition: about 98 percent of Congressional incumbents get re-elected. Soft money can help challengers compete with incumbents. Parties make sure soft money ends up where it's needed most." [54]

Although the soft money ban was promoted as an anti-corruption measure, some people believe that the soft money system actually *decreases* the possibility of corruption by isolating elected officials from political contributors. Many people believe that, regardless of campaign-finance legislation, politicians will continue to find new ways of financing their campaigns. If these methods were to rely exclusively on contributions directly to candidates, politicians would be more likely to feel obligated to these contributors. On the other hand, under the soft money system, when contributions come to a national political party, which can use the funds for any of hundreds of candidates, the chance that any one candidate will feel obligated to the contributor is reduced. Calling soft money contributions "a buffer against corruption," Samples writes, "The winners are beholden to their party and not to individual donors. Soft money actually is less of a danger than money given directly to a candidate's campaign." [55]

> • Do you believe that the soft money system reduced the chance of corruption? Wouldn't decreasing the amount of money overall do a better job of preventing corruption?

Another major problem with banning soft money is that, while the ban might limit the influence of corporations and wealthy individuals, the ban will allow others even greater influence in the political process. For example, even though the soft money ban covers labor unions, the Cato Institute's Doug Bandow believes that the ban would actually give unions an unfair advantage over other interest groups, such as corporations, because labor unions "often deploy legions of volunteers" for campaign and election activities.[56]

Similarly, it is undisputed that the news media, especially television and newspapers, have an enormous influence over the outcome of elections. The media can have a huge impact on voters' choices by endorsing particular candidates, or by running coverage favorable or unfavorable to particular candidates— such as reporting just before the 2000 election that George W. Bush had been arrested many years previously for drunk driving. By limiting political parties' financial resources to run advertisements, writes Tom Bethell, enforcement of a soft money ban "would increase the media's power by restricting alternative sources of information."[57]

> • **Does the media have too much influence in deciding elections?**

Contributions by individuals are an essential part of the political process.

Even some supporters of moderate campaign reforms, including President George W. Bush, believe that Congress went too far in banning "soft money" contributions by individuals. When he signed the BCRA into law, the president stated: "[T]he bill does have flaws. Certain provisions present serious constitutional concerns. In particular, [the BCRA] goes farther than I originally proposed by preventing all individuals, not just unions and corporations, from making donations to political parties. . . . I believe individual freedom to participate in elections should be expanded, not diminished. . . ."[58] In President Bush's view, the problem with corporate and union "soft money" was that individual shareholders of corporations and members of unions did not have the power to control how the corporate or union leadership spent money rightly belonging to shareholders and union members. He viewed this as an assault on the individual right to make one's own political choices.

Opponents of campaign finance restrictions believe that placing restrictions on the amount of money that an individual can contribute to candidates of his or her choice limits that person's participation in the democratic process. For example, while a person might not have time to go door-to-door canvassing on behalf of a political candidate, the person might have enough money to donate to the candidate's campaign to help the candidate hire canvassers. By limiting individual citizens' ability to make campaign contributions, state and federal election laws limit their citizens' voice in politics.

While many criticized the role of out-of-state Jewish contributors in helping to defeat Earl Hilliard and Cynthia McKinney, two African-American politicians in the Deep South, others thought that the defeat was a lesson in democracy. Michael Barone writes that the reason Hilliard and McKinney lost was not simply because out-of-state contributors had supported their challengers, Artur Davis and Denise Majette; rather: "Majette and Davis couldn't win unless their issue stands were acceptable to most primary voters. You can spend a lot of money and still lose if the product you're selling isn't acceptable."[59] In Barone's opinion, Hilliard and McKinney lost because they took extreme positions on Israel, terrorism, and other issues; out-of-state contributions merely helped the challengers publicize these positions.

• **Can massive campaign spending help a candidate whose positions are unpopular with voters?**

Without limits on the sources or amounts of donations permitted to political candidates, it is easy for some wealthy people to exert a great deal of influence over the campaign process. One major financial supporter of political campaigns has been Stanley S. Hubbard (seen here), president of Hubbard Broadcasting. In 2002, he donated over $200,000 to political campaigns, making him the twenty-seventh largest donor in the country that year.

FROM THE BENCH

Justice Thomas: Campaign Finance Reform Violates the First Amendment

Political speech is the primary object of First Amendment protection. . . . The Founders sought to protect the rights of individuals to engage in political speech because a self-governing people depends upon the free exchange of political information. And that free exchange should receive the most protection when it matters the most — during campaigns for elective office. . . .

For nearly half a century, this Court has extended First Amendment protection to a multitude of forms of "speech," such as making false defamatory statements, filing lawsuits, dancing nude, exhibiting drive-in movies with nudity, burning flags, and wearing military uniforms. Not surprisingly, the Courts of Appeals have followed our lead and concluded that the First Amendment protects, for example, begging, shouting obscenities, erecting tables on a sidewalk, and refusing to wear a necktie. . . . Whatever the proper status of such activities under the First Amendment, I am confident that they are less integral to the functioning of our Republic than campaign contributions. . . .

The decision of individuals to speak through contributions . . . is entirely reasonable. . . . Campaign organizations offer a ready-built, convenient means of communicating for donors wishing to support and amplify political messages. Furthermore, the leader of the organization — the candidate — has a strong self-interest in efficiently expending funds in a manner that maximizes the power of the messages the contributor seeks to disseminate. Individual citizens understandably realize that they "may add more to political discourse by giving rather than spending, if the donee is able to put the funds to more productive use than can the individual." . . .

Even for the affluent, the added costs in money or time of taking out a newspaper advertisement, handing out leaflets on the street, or standing in front of one's house with a hand-held sign may make the difference between participating and not participating in some public debate. . . .

Source: *Nixon v. Shrink Missouri PAC*, No. 98-963 (January 24, 2000) (Thomas, J., dissenting)

Restrictions on political contributions violate the First Amendment.

Some people have taken the passage of the BCRA as a means of challenging one of the central holdings of *Buckley* v. *Valeo*— that the federal government, acting consistently with the First Amendment, may limit campaign contributions more closely than it may regulate expenditures on political speech. Many people have challenged the Court's distinction between political speech and political spending, because it is clear that political speech costs money. Attorney Erik S. Jaffe and the Cato Institute's Robert Levy believe that it is inconsistent to believe that the Constitution protects the exercise of a particular right but not the payment of money to exercise that right. They write: "The right to speak . . . encompasses the right to pay for speech . . . just as the right to legal counsel encompasses the right to hire a lawyer, and the right to free exercise of religion includes the right to contribute to the church of one's choice."[60]

Many opponents of campaign finance restrictions also believe that the soft money ban is too broad because it places too many restrictions on the speech of political parties. The purported rationale behind the soft money ban is to limit election communications—something the Court held was constitutional in *Buckley*. However, the soft money ban goes much further than that. The ban makes it much more difficult for political parties to engage in legitimate party activities, such as voter registration drives.

Opponents of the soft money ban believe the underlying motivation of "reformers"—those trying to eliminate corruption—is suspect. They feel that there is no real proof that soft money has led to any specific improper acts, and that the so-called "perception" of corruption is not a valid enough reason to limit contributions to parties. In a lawsuit challenging the constitutionality of the BCRA, the Cato Institute and the Institute of Justice argued that, while fighting "actual

Trend in Reported Faith in Elections, 1964–1996

National Election Studies (NES) sample averages for presidential
election years, adjusted for panel status and date of interview

The continued prevalence of controversy within campaign
ancing and continued voter fraud has led many Americans to
se faith in the electoral system. This chart shows the downward
end in voter confidence in the election process from 1964
1996.

corruption" is an important goal, the federal government should not suppress political expression—such as soft money contributions—that have not been proven to lead to actual corruption. In an *amicus* (friend-of-the-court) brief, the groups argued: "[T]he proper answer to such misperception is either more speech, the election of candidates voluntarily practicing the public's notion of virtue, or, ultimately, a constitutional amendment if the existing system cannot hold the public's confidence."[61] In other words, if the public thinks that politicians are corrupt, then the answer is for the public to vote the politicians out of office; the answer is not for the government to suppress political debate.

> • **Do you agree that spending money is a form of "free speech" protected by the Constitution?**

Though Congress passed the Bipartisan Campaign Reform Act of 2002 with widespread support, opponents have challenged the law as unconstitutional. Not everyone agrees that there is too much money in politics. Many believe that the party system is essential to democracy and that parties need money to survive. Similarly, campaign contributions allow people to express their political views.

The Government Should Regulate Television Advertisements and Campaign Coverage

In the months leading up to the 1988 presidential election, Democrat Michael Dukakis was jockeying for position against Republican Vice President George H.W. Bush. However, the Dukakis campaign fell apart after a series of television commercials attacked his record as governor of Massachusetts. The first advertisement, sponsored by an independent political action committee—not the Bush campaign—introduced Americans to a person who would become permanently linked with Michael Dukakis: Willie Horton.

Portraying Dukakis as "soft on crime," the advertisements showed the mug shot of Horton, a convicted murderer who had received numerous short "furloughs" from prison under a program that Dukakis strongly supported. During one such furlough, Horton kidnapped and assaulted a young couple, raping the woman. The ads generated a great deal of media

Gov 'gave pardons to 21 drug dealers'

Will Dukakis Turn Gun Owners Into Criminals... While Murderers Go Free?

The Most Soft-on-Crime Governor in Massachusetts History
Is a Leading Advocate of Gun Control

Gun Owner Magazine quotes Dukakis as saying in 1986, **"I don't believe in people owning guns, only the police and military. And I'm going to do everything I can to disarm this state."** In 1976 Dukakis supported a (losing) statewide referendum which would have done just that. Dukakis has called for **federal registration** of all concealable handguns and has written, "... the solution to the problem of gun-inflicted violence must come at the national level."

Michael Dukakis talks about fighting crime, but there is a big gap between the *rhetoric* and the *record*. Maybe that's why the **Boston Police Patrolman's Association unanimously endorsed George Bush for President.**

While trying to deny the citizens of Massachusetts the right to defend themselves, Dukakis has put more convicted criminals on the streets than any governor in his state's history.

• He has used his gubernatorial pardoning power to commute the sentences of *44 convicted murderers*—a record for the state of Massachusetts.

• He has vetoed and continues to oppose the death penalty *under any circumstances*, even for cop-killers, drug kingpins and traitors.

• He *opposes* mandatory sentences for hard-core criminals but *supports* mandatory sentences for anyone caught with an unregistered gun *of any kind*.

Dukakis has also presided over and actively endorsed the *most liberal prisoner furlough program in America*, the only one in the nation releasing prisoners sentenced to life without parole.

• On average, in the state of Massachusetts, one convicted first degree murderer was released *every day* over the last seven years.

• Since the beginning of Dukakis' second term as Governor, 1,905 furloughs have been granted to first degree murderers and at least 4,459 furloughs to second degree murderers. He has given 2,565 furloughs to drug offenders.

• In 1986 alone, Dukakis gave 1,229 furloughs to sex crime offenders, including 220 to persons charged with *six or more* sex offenses.

• Today 85 violent felons from Massachusetts are on the loose in America—set free on furloughs, they never bothered to come back.

One of the most controversial attack ad campaigns was used in the 1988 presidential election. Supporters of Republican candidate George H.W. Bush used opponent Michael Dukakis's past grants of furloughs to convicted felons to demonstrate that Dukakis was soft on crime. The ads told the story of how one inmate, Willie Horton, committed a rape while out on a furlough permitted by Dukakis.

coverage, with Horton's victims appearing on a number of high-profile television programs. Soon afterward, Bush's campaign launched its own set of advertisements, attacking Dukakis's record on crime without mentioning Horton specifically.

In *Checkbook Democracy*, political science professor Darrell M. West writes that the two-pronged attack—with an independent group running ads linking Dukakis to Horton, and the

Bush campaign running ads with general criticism of Dukakis's policy—worked extremely well for Bush. He was able to paint a very negative picture of Dukakis without being criticized for running a negative campaign. More significantly, West writes, the ads benefited Bush by "arous[ing] racial fears" among Americans: "Republicans had picked the perfect racial offense, that of a black felon raping a white woman." [62]

Bush won the election by a comfortable margin, but many question whether his tactics were fair. Certainly, it was a legitimate concern that the furlough program Dukakis supported had allowed a convicted murderer with a life sentence to leave prison and commit other crimes. However, many felt that the proper way for Bush to inform voters of this concern would have been to take up the issue in a debate, or at least to deliver the criticisms in his own voice without hiding behind an anonymous attack ad.

> • Was it important for voters to know about the furlough program? Is it ever unfair to attack another person with "the truth"?

Attack ads harm democracy by distorting the real issues.

Although the "Willie Horton" advertising campaign was not the first occurrence of negative campaigning in American politics, some people think that the advertisements opened the door for a new style of campaigning in which politicians ignored the real issues and instead attacked the other candidate's personal character or distorted the other candidate's positions.

In Montana's 2002 senatorial race, Republican challenger Mike Taylor pulled out of the race after the Democratic incumbent candidate, Senator Max Baucus, ran a controversial television ad. The advertisement accused Taylor of running a "student loan scam" during the 1980s. Taylor admitted that his hairstyling schools had made some bookkeeping errors and had repaid the federal government $27,000, but he said that he had admitted his errors and made good on the discrepancy and that the settlement in the case did not include any admission of wrongdoing. Therefore, Taylor said, the accusation of his running a "student loan scam" was very misleading.

Even more misleading, Taylor's campaign manager told the *Great Falls Tribune*, was that the ad "insinuates that Mike Taylor is a gay hairdresser." As described by the article, the ad shows actual video footage "of a bearded Taylor from nearly 20 years ago, dressed in flamboyant 1970s-era clothing and applying face cream to a male model." [63] While the ad showed actual footage of the television show on which Taylor actually appeared, many attacked the Democratic campaign for appealing to anti-gay prejudices of conservative Montanans, much as the Willie Horton ads had appealed to racial prejudices in 1988. With damaging commercials such as this, once the cat is out of the bag, it is difficult to control the damage. After withdrawing from the race, Taylor said that he would have had to "blanket the airwaves with slime" to counteract Baucus's accusations of fraud and insinuations of homosexuality. [64]

Another criticism that many people make is that attack ads are often designed as an anonymous attack on a person's character. One of the biggest criticisms of the Willie Horton advertising campaign was that the advertisements attacked Michael Dukakis by appealing to people's racial prejudices. Had George Bush attempted such tactics, the public might have branded him a racist, but because the ads were relatively anonymous, Bush benefited from the advertisements without being linked with their message.

In the view of many people, the First Amendment was designed to protect public debate, not anonymous attacks on a person's character. For years, Congress has carefully regulated campaign advertisements, requiring that the advertisements disclose the source of their funding. (In the 1976 *Buckley* v. *Valeo* decision, the Supreme Court ruled that the federal government could regulate any advertisement that "expressly advocates the election or defeat of a clearly identified candidate.")[65] However, in the years leading up to the passage of the BCRA, many groups skirted this requirement by running advertisements attacking a candidate without explicitly advising people to vote against him or her. Such advertisements escaped federal regulation of campaign advertising; therefore, the sponsors of the ad were not identified.

Although the sponsors of such advertisements have claimed that they are "issue ads," they are often campaign advertisements that have very little to do with issues. Arguing in support of the BCRA's ban on "sham issue advertisements," a coalition of former ACLU leaders gave an example of an anonymous "issue" ad that

THE LETTER OF THE LAW

Bipartisan Campaign Reform Act's Definition of Campaign Advertisements.

(3) ELECTIONEERING COMMUNICATION.—For purposes of this subsection—
   (A) IN GENERAL.—
      (i) The term "electioneering communication" means any broadcast, cable, or satellite communication which—
      (I) refers to a clearly identified candidate for Federal office;
      (II) is made within—
         (aa) 60 days before a general, special, or run-off election for the office sought by the candidate; or
         (bb) 30 days before a primary or preference election, or a convention or caucus of a political party that has authority to nominate a candidate, for the office sought by the candidate; and
      (III) in the case of a communication which refers to a candidate for an office other than President or Vice President, is targeted to the relevant electorate.

Source: Bipartisan Campaign Reform Act, Pub. L. No. 107-155 (March 22, 2002).

Attack ads often try to use statements from a candidate's past career to discredit him or her. The problem is that these statements are often taken out of context, and it can be difficult for voters to determine the truth.

was clearly a campaign advertisement—it began running two weeks before the congressional election:

> Who is Bill Yellowtail? He preaches family values but took a swing at his wife. . . . He talks law and order . . . but is himself a convicted felon. And though he talks about protecting children, Yellowtail failed to make his own child support payments—then voted against child support enforcement. Call Bill Yellowtail. Tell him to support family values.[66]

Despite its obvious attempt to influence an election, the sponsors of this advertisement claimed that it was not a campaign ad subject to federal regulation. The former ACLU leaders argued, "The increased use of such advertisements has undermined the [law] . . . and allowed other individuals and entities to fund . .

advertisements without disclosing their identities or providing the electorate with crucial information regarding funding sources to enable the electorate to make informed federal election choices."[67] Without such a ban, the KKK, for example, could advertise in favor of a certain candidate and the public would never know.

> • Should politicians have to stand behind what they say about the other candidate? Does freedom of speech apply to anonymous speech?

The BCRA included measures limiting attack ads, extending the definition of "electioneering communications" subject to federal regulations to include any advertisement referring to a "clearly identified candidate for Federal office" within 30 days of a primary election or 60 days of a general election.[68] Supporters of the legislation hope that the provision will close the loophole in federal election law that allowed anonymous advertisers to attack candidates for office using "sham issue ads."

However, the debate over attack ads appears to be far from over, even with the passage of the BCRA. Several groups have challenged the specific provisions dealing with attack ads in court. Therefore—as with campaign finance reform—supporters of limits on attacks ads have found themselves defending the law, and they might have to draft a replacement law if the courts invalidate portions of the BCRA.

> • Is it wise to restrict people from running advertisements revealing that a candidate for office has been convicted of a crime?

The proliferation of television advertisement interferes with meaningful election coverage.

To many campaign reformers, the problem of television advertising is not limited to attack ads that distort the issues. Another problem, campaign reformers say, is that lucrative advertisement sales encourage stations to provide even less coverage of campaign issues. Rather than having local news programs explore political issues in greater detail or setting aside time for debates, television stations simply sell more advertising time to politicians. As Senator Russell Feingold commented:

> Although broadcast advertising is one of the most effective forms of communication in our democracy, it also diminishes the quality of our electoral process in two ways. First, broadcasters often fail to provide adequate coverage to the issues in elections, focusing instead on the horse race, if they cover elections at all. Second, the extraordinarily high cost of advertising time fuels the insatiable need for candidates to spend more and more time fundraising instead of talking with voters. These two problems interact to undermine the great promise that television has for promoting democratic discourse in our country.[69]

Many people believe it might be possible for candidates to make some valid points on certain issues during a 30-second television advertisement. For example, Candidate A might run an ad criticizing Candidate B for her past votes to raise taxes. However, people who see the ad would not know the whole story. Perhaps Candidate B voted to raise taxes to rescue failing public schools, or for some other reason that voters might support. Most political issues are extremely complicated and cannot be discussed in a 30-second commercial.

Journalist Jeffrey H. Birnbaum believes that voters would learn much more and be able to make informed decisions if they watched programming in which candidates discussed the issues in more depth—such as "minidebates, interviews, or even straightforward statements read on the air by the candidates themselves . . . programming that would inform voters about the upcoming election by using the candidates themselves."[70] As a successful example of such a strategy, Birnbaum cites the surprise election of former professional wrestler Jesse "The Body" Ventura as Minnesota's governor. After television stations in Minnesota's largest cities aired two-minute messages by the candidates and the League of Women voters arranged a debate that was carried statewide, Ventura beat both the Democratic and Republican candidates in an election that attracted many new voters to the polls. Birnbaum called what happened in Minnesota a "model of how to avoid superficial TV coverage of a campaign."[71]

Unfortunately, say reformers, in most of the rest of the country, broadcasters are not so willing to carry debates and other programs examining issue in depth. Senator Feingold lamented, "[O]nly 18% of gubernatorial, senatorial and congressional debates held in 2000 were televised by network TV and an additional 18% were covered by PBS or small independent stations. More than 63% were not televised at all. This is shocking in a democracy that depends on information and open debate."[72]

> • **Should television stations be required to cover debates if people aren't interested in watching them? Does it make sense to make all stations carry the debates at the same time?**

Free airtime and televised debates for candidates would benefit voters.

The answer to the lack of meaningful candidate programming, say campaign reformers, is to require broadcasters to carry the type of programming that the Minnesota stations carried when Jesse Ventura was running for office. To that end, Senators McCain and Feingold, following up on the BCRA, have proposed that television stations be required to carry two hours of political programming per week in the weeks leading up to a federal election. Without such a requirement, they argue, most stations would continue to shun meaningful election coverage. In economic terms, it makes sense for profit-seeking television stations to sell advertising time to candidates, since the less "free" coverage the stations provide, the more advertising spots they can sell.

To campaign reformers, however, the issue is not so simple. Citing the principle that the airwaves are a public trust, they argue that the stations have a duty to provide programming in the public interest. Senator McCain has argued: "[There is a] long history of requiring broadcasters to serve the public interest in exchange for the privilege of obtaining an exclusive license to use a scarce public resource: the electromagnetic spectrum."[73] Each television set sold has a limited number of channels that can pick up television broadcasts through the airwaves—as opposed to through cable television. Television channels correspond to different "wavelengths" of electromagnetic radiation—the same type of invisible radiation that carries radio stations and cell phone and cordless phone conversations. Television stations do not "use up" a particular wavelength; in theory, there could be ten stations in one town, all broadcasting on Channel Five. The obvious problem is that—if there were ten stations on the same channel—nobody could watch any of the stations because they would all interfere with each other.

Therefore, the federal government grants each television station an exclusive license to use a particular channel in a particular area. In the words of Senator Feingold, "The public owns the airwaves and licenses them to broadcasters. Broadcasters pay nothing for their use of this scarce and very valuable public resource. Their only 'payment' is a promise to meet public interest standards, a promise that often goes unfulfilled."[74] Throughout the history of television, the government has used the public interest rationale to require that television stations air "public service announcements," such as reminders from the fire department to check smoke detector batteries. The same rationale explains why broadcast television stations have agreed not to use explicit language or graphic sex and violence.

- **Should television stations be able to broadcast whatever they want to?**

Supporters of the free airtime proposals believe that the public interest rationale strongly supports free airtime for political candidates. They note that the imposition on broadcasters—two hours per week for six weeks—is very reasonable compared to the immense value of a broadcast license. In the words of Senator McCain, "The burden imposed on broadcasters pales in comparison to the enormous value of the spectrum, which recent estimates suggest is worth as much as $367 billion."[75]

Supreme Court Rules That Scarcity of Broadcast Spectrum Allows Regulation of Radio and Television

Although broadcasting is clearly a medium affected by a First Amendment interest ... differences in the characteristics of new media justify differences in the First Amendment standards applied to them. ...

[B]ecause the frequencies reserved for public broadcasting were limited in number, it was essential for the Government to tell some applicants that they could not broadcast at all because there was room for only a few.

Where there are substantially more individuals who want to broadcast than there are frequencies to allocate, it is idle to posit an unabridgeable First Amendment right to broadcast comparable to the right of every individual to speak, write, or publish. If 100 persons want broadcast licenses but there are only 10 frequencies to allocate, all of them may have the same "right" to a license; but if there is to be any effective communication by radio, only a few can be licensed and the rest must be barred from the airwaves. ...

[As] far as the First Amendment is concerned those who are licensed stand no better than those to whom licenses are refused. A license permits broadcasting, but the licensee has no constitutional right to be the one who holds the license or to monopolize a radio frequency to the exclusion of his fellow citizens. There is nothing in the First Amendment which prevents the Government from requiring a licensee to share his frequency with others and to conduct himself as a proxy or fiduciary with obligations to present those views and voices which are representative of his community and which would otherwise, by necessity, be barred from the airwaves. ...

[The] people as a whole retain their interest in free speech by radio and their collective right to have the medium function consistently with the ends and purposes of the First Amendment. It is the right of the viewers and listeners, not the right of the broadcasters, which is paramount. ... It is the purpose of the First Amendment to preserve an uninhibited marketplace of ideas in which truth will ultimately prevail, rather than to countenance monopolization of that market, whether it be by the Government itself or a private licensee.

Source: *Red Lion Broadcasting Co. v. FCC*, 395 U.S. 367 (1969)

Supporters note that free airtime has been successful in places in which it has been tried. Ric Bainter and Paul Lhevine have praised Seattle's efforts to convince television stations to air the "Video Voter Guide," in which each candidate has three minutes to address the public. They write, "Seattle continues to lead the way in campaign finance work and sets a clear example for others to follow."[76]

Broadcasters and opponents of campaign reform have attacked laws restricting attack ads and proposals to give candidates free airtime on First Amendment grounds. Although the First Amendment does prohibit Congress from passing any laws "abridging the freedom of speech," campaign reformers have maintained that regulating the use of a public resource as valuable as the airwaves does not impinge upon free speech. Rather, it is similar to requiring people to obtain a permit to hold an event in a public place—something that the Supreme Court has said is not a violation of First Amendment rights.

- **Does the availability of hundreds of cable channels lessen the "value" of the broadcast spectrum?**

Many people attribute low voter turnout to the way campaigns are typically conducted: 30-second ads attacking one of the candidates, with most voters learning very little about the real issues. Numerous groups have challenged the constitutionality of the BCRA's limits on attack ads, but campaign reformers believe that change is absolutely necessary. They would like to see more in-depth campaign coverage on television, and they even have suggested that television stations be required to provide candidates with free airtime.

Government Restrictions on Television Advertisements and Programming Are Unconstitutional and Undemocratic

To members of Congress, the BCRA's limitations on attack ads seemed desirable or necessary. However, to many civil libertarians, the restrictions on attack ads are a blatant violation of the First Amendment's guarantee of freedom of speech. Together with free airtime for political candidates, such government control of the airwaves reminds civil libertarians of oppressive dictatorships in which political dissent is silenced. Some have gone so far as to compare efforts to regulate campaign advertisements and media coverage to George Orwell's novel *1984*, in which two-way televisions monitored people's every move and the Thought Police sought to suppress any dissenting ideas.

Though not everyone takes such a drastic view of restrictions on issue ads or proposals to provide free airtime to candidates, opposition has come from all parts of the political spectrum.

Liberal groups such as the ACLU and conservative groups such as the National Rifle Association (NRA) have united to challenge the BCRA in court, and they likely will challenge any subsequent legislation limiting issue advertisements that might result from the court challenge.

Maybe the Willie Horton ad campaign was not an example of politics at its very best. It certainly was not the first example of "dirty" campaigning, though. Florida's 1950 senatorial election provides perhaps the most humorous example of dirty campaigning. Reportedly, George Smathers called incumbent Claude Pepper a "shameless extrovert" who "matriculated" while he was in college and practiced "celibacy" before marriage. These claims were absolutely true and absolutely innocuous—but they sounded dirty to people who were unfamiliar with the terms. (An extrovert is simply a person with an outgoing personality; to matriculate means to attend school; and celibacy basically means not having sexual intercourse.) Taking advantage of large numbers of voters with low education levels, Smathers defeated Pepper.

Today, the media would have exposed Smathers's ruse, but more frequently, candidates rely upon attack ads that make much more controversial statements and often include those sponsored by independent groups. Although many senators and representatives express their disgust with anonymous television ads attacking their character and politics, many supporters believe that political pressure is a necessary part of the political process.

> • **Is it fair to attack someone with the truth by using words that convey the opposite meaning?**

Restrictions on "attack ads" favor some viewpoints over others.

A major criticism of the BCRA's restrictions on television ads mentioning a candidate's name is that, by limiting the voice of corporations, labor unions, and interest groups such as the NRA and ACLU, the law gives others—especially the media—an unfair amount of influence. Therefore, although ads are limited, news stories are not. In a brief challenging the BCRA's constitutionality, the NRA argued that, while "a nonprofit advocacy group funded by individual membership dues cannot purchase time," media corporations can endorse candidates of their choice: "Rupert Murdoch's News Corporation, for example, will be free to endorse or blackball candidates at will. Indeed, News Corporation will be free to produce a weekly television program such as *American Candidate*, [promoting] presidential candidates who have been selected by the News Corporation." [77]

The NRA also protested that the BCRA banned ads by membership organizations but not ads placed by wealthy individuals. In so doing, the NRA argued, the BCRA stifles the voice of ordinary citizens: "[T]he aggregated wealth that the NRA accumulates corresponds with its members' support for its political ideas. If the NRA's voice is loud and reverberates through the halls of Congress, it is precisely because the organization is the *collective voice* of millions of Americans speaking in unison." [78]

Congress garnered public support for restrictions on "attack ads" largely by creating a backlash against so-called "special interest groups"—such as the NRA and ACLU—that have allegedly gained too much influence in politics. However, some have questioned this characterization, saying that these groups represent all parts of the political spectrum. As the Media Institute argued in a friend-of-the-court brief in a lawsuit challenging the BCRA:

> Although proponents of campaign regulation argue that intervention is needed to prevent one-sided domination of political dialogue, the facts show that citizens with political views falling on opposite ends of the ideological spectrum and from vastly different socio-economic backgrounds engage in issue advocacy. . . . [I]ndependent organizations of all stripes use the broadcast media to express their views on public policy issues, including healthcare, the environment,

education, social security, international affairs, national
defense, abortion, taxation and gun control. . . . These groups
are not homogeneous; they do not uniformly advance the
same political agenda; "liberals" and "conservatives" alike
sponsor issue advertisements.[79]

Law professor Lillian BeVier rejects the idea that issue
advertisements give any group "undue influence." She writes,
"There is . . . no constitutional warrant or means for calibrating
what constitutes 'undue' influence. . . . We have no constitutional
Goldilocks to say when the amount of influence possessed
by advocates of particular positions is 'just right.'"[80] What
BeVier means by her Goldilocks analogy is that the Constitution
guarantees freedom of speech and does not allow the government to favor one type of speech over another.

- **Isn't the media *supposed* to have opinions on political issues?**

Restrictions on "attack ads" silence political dissent.

People have also criticized the BCRA's ban on attack ads as being
overly broad. Because there are limitless ways to word a political
advertisement, it would be impossible for the government to set
standards as to what constitutes an attack ad and what does not.
On the other hand, passing judgment on ads on a case-by-case
basis would require government officials to act as censors,
gutting the spirit of the First Amendment's protection of free
speech. Because the government cannot describe what exactly
constitutes an "attack ad" and what does not, the BCRA took
a much broader approach, banning all ads that reference an
identified candidate within 60 days of a general election or
30 days of a primary election.

Opponents of advertising restrictions say that the BCRA's
blanket ban is unconstitutional because it is "overbroad," meaning that it bans more speech than is absolutely necessary. Even if

it were legitimate for Congress to ban "attack ads"—which critics deny—the BCRA's ban does much more.

At the heart of freedom of speech is the ability to criticize the government without fearing retribution or having the government modify what is said. Ruling that an Alabama public official could not collect money from *The New York Times*, the

FROM THE BENCH

Supreme Court Rules That Constitution Protects Criticism of Public Officials.

The general proposition that freedom of expression upon public questions is secured by the First Amendment has long been settled by our decisions. The constitutional safeguard, we have said, "was fashioned to assure unfettered interchange of ideas for the bringing about of political and social changes desired by the people." . . . The First Amendment, said Judge Learned Hand, "presupposes that right conclusions are more likely to be gathered out of a multitude of tongues, than through any kind of authoritative selection. To many this is, and always will be, folly; but we have staked upon it our all." . . .

[There has been] a profound national commitment to the principle that debate on public issues should be uninhibited, robust, and wide-open, and that it may well include vehement, caustic, and sometimes unpleasantly sharp attacks on government and public officials.…The present advertisement, as an expression of grievance and protest on one of the major public issues of our time, would seem clearly to qualify for the constitutional protection. The question is whether it forfeits that protection by the falsity of some of its factual statements and by its alleged defamation of respondent.…

Injury to official reputation affords no more warrant for repressing speech that would otherwise be free than does factual error. Where judicial officers are involved, this Court has held that concern for the dignity and …reputation of the courts does not justify the punishment as criminal contempt of criticism of the judge or his decision.…This is true even though the utterance contains "half-truths" and "misinformation." …

If neither factual error nor defamatory content suffices to remove the constitutional shield from criticism of official conduct, the combination of the two elements is no less inadequate. This is the lesson to be drawn from the great controversy over

Court noted that the United States has "a profound national commitment to the principle that debate on public issues should be uninhibited, robust, and wide-open, and that it may well include vehement, caustic, and sometimes unpleasantly sharp attacks on government and public officials."[81] In that case, an advertisement in the paper contained some minor inaccuracies

the Sedition Act of 1798 . . . which first crystallized a national awareness of the central meaning of the First Amendment. . . . That statute made it a crime, punishable by a $5,000 fine and five years in prison, "if any person shall write, print, utter or publish . . . any false, scandalous and malicious writing or writings against the government of the United States, or either house of the Congress, . . . or the President, . . . with intent to defame . . . or to bring them, or either of them, into contempt or disrepute; or to excite against them, or either or any of them, the hatred of the good people of the United States." . . .

Although the Sedition Act was never tested in this Court, the attack upon its validity has carried the day in the court of history. Fines levied in its prosecution were repaid by Act of Congress on the ground that it was unconstitutional. . . . Jefferson, as President, pardoned those who had been convicted and sentenced under the Act and remitted their fines, stating: "I discharged every person under punishment or prosecution under the sedition law, because I considered, and now consider, that law to be a nullity, as absolute and as palpable as if Congress had ordered us to fall down and worship a golden image." . . . These views reflect a broad consensus that the Act, because of the restraint it imposed upon criticism of government and public officials, was inconsistent with the First Amendment.

The constitutional guarantees require, we think, a federal rule that prohibits a public official from recovering damages for a defamatory falsehood relating to his official conduct unless he proves that the statement was made . . . with "actual malice"—that is, with knowledge that it was false or with reckless disregard of whether it was false or not.

Source: *New York Times Co.* v. *Sullivan,* 376 U.S. 254 (1964)

regarding the official, but the Court overturned a lower court's libel award in the official's favor.

> • **Would you want to live in a country where it is illegal to criticize the government?**

Some groups have complained that the restrictions on so-called "sham issue ads" have the potential to interfere substantially with legitimate issue discussion. Often, pending legislation is discussed in public by reference to the bill's sponsors. For example, before its passage into law, BCRA was called the "McCain-Feingold Bill." In challenging the restrictions, the ACLU argued: "[T]he blackout periods imposed by BCRA—60 days before a general election and 30 days before a primary—are often periods of intense legislative activity. During election years, the candidates stake out positions on virtually all of the controversial issues of the day."[82]

More importantly, because our elected officials are frequently candidates for re-election, restrictions on campaign advertising simultaneously prevent citizens from criticizing their elected officials. To many, this type of restriction on political speech is not at all what the Supreme Court envisioned when it issued the *Buckley* v. *Valeo* ruling. In its 2002 court challenge of the BCRA, the ACLU—citing the *Buckley* decision—argued:

> The Court recognized that efforts to regulate campaign speech would present a serious risk of curtailing the capacity of citizens, as individuals and in association with others, to express freely their views on important matters of public policy and on the behavior of public officials in the conduct of government affairs. . . . It is not that there is an inherent distinction between issue speech and electoral advocacy. Quite the contrary, as the Court recognized: "For the distinction between discussion of issues and candidates and advocacy of election or defeat of candidates may often dissolve in practical application. Candidates, especially incumbents, are intimately tied to public issues involving legislative proposals and governmental actions. . . ."[83]

Recently, many opponents of campaign restrictions have begun to criticize the rule that grew out of *Buckley* v. *Valeo*— that the federal government could regulate any advertisement that "expressly advocates the election or defeat of a clearly identified candidate."[84] Attorney Erik S. Jaffe and the Cato Institute's Robert Levy have argued that, not only are the BCRA's restrictions on sham issue ads unconstitutional, but any other federal regulation of campaign advertisements also are unconstitutional. They write, "When a corporation or union expressly advocates the election or defeat of a candidate, that act—no less than issue advocacy—lies at the heart of the First Amendment."[85]

Similarly, opponents of the BCRA's advertising restrictions believe that anonymous attack ads are a legitimate type of political discussion. Anonymous criticisms certainly have a lengthy history in American politics. For example, Benjamin Franklin frequently wrote under fictional names while criticizing Pennsylvania's colonial government. The ACLU has argued that requiring advertisements to disclose the source of their funding "would violate longstanding First Amendment rules designed to protect anonymous political speech and the right to associate with controversial political groups."[86]

- Is a "blackout" period an acceptable solution for preserving freedom of speech? Could the government limit abortion protests on the anniversary of *Roe* v. *Wade*?

Government regulation of TV election coverage is unconstitutional and undemocratic.

After passage of the BCRA, campaign reformers such as Senators McCain and Feingold turned their attention to proposals that would require broadcasters to give politicians free access to the broadcasts of privately owned television stations. They argued that requiring television stations to provide free airtime to candidates and to carry political debates would help "clean up" politics.

They introduced the Political Campaign Broadcast Activity Improvements Act, which requires television stations—as a condition of retaining their government license—to air two hours per week of programming such as debates, interviews, or candidate statements in the weeks prior to a federal election.

Civil libertarians have used many of the same arguments they used to challenge BCRA in court to oppose free airtime proposals. Many view free airtime legislation as a "catch-22." On the one hand, allowing free airtime to all candidates would distract people from the important issues because "fringe" candidates would detract viewers' attention from "legitimate" candidates. Critics of systems that give public support to candidates—such as campaign funding or free airtime—have denounced providing benefits to candidates such as "convicted felon Lyndon LaRouche, John Hagelin of the Natural Law Party (which advocates greater use of transcendental meditation . . .), and Lenora Fulani of the New Alliance Party (a socialist party that has been accused of engaging in cult-type brainwashing)." [87]

On the other hand, it would be difficult for a free airtime bill to exclude so-called "fringe" candidates, because doing so would amount to government censorship of controversial viewpoints. Former Delaware Governor Pete du Pont criticized an earlier proposal that would provide free airtime to "ballot-worthy candidates." He questioned, for example, whether the pro-segregation "Strom Thurmond and the Dixiecrats in 1948" would have been considered ballot-worthy. [88]

> • **Do you support the idea of free airtime? Would you be interested in actually watching the programming?**

Many civil libertarians believe that it is dangerous for government to take control of private industry, even temporarily, and that the danger is especially significant when government takes control of the media. Edward Crane of the Cato Institute writes: "'Airwaves' is a misnomer. Radio and television broadcasting utilizes electromagnetic radiation, which occurs in a

In 1948, Strom Thurmond ran for president of the United States on a platform that demanded the continuance of racial segregation in public places. Despite his controversial views, Thurmond eventually won a Senate seat and remained there for decades, which demonstrates how difficult it can often be to unseat an incumbent politician.

state of nature. . . . Turning [it] into communication requires a significant investment [like] turning naturally occurring iron ore into steel. . . ."[89] In Crane's opinion, television is a private industry that the government should not be able to "commandeer" for campaigning purposes.

As could be imagined, broadcasters have also voiced strong objections to free airtime proposals. Broadcasters feel that such requirements harm them financially and interfere with editorial control. Much like their opposition to restrictions on advertising, civil libertarians believe that government control of the airwaves threatens free speech, especially during critical campaign times.

Part of broadcasters' objection to free airtime proposals is practical. Broadcast television, and, to a lesser extent, cable television, rely on advertising revenue to make a profit. Political advertising is an important source of revenue, and though campaign reformers have accused broadcasters of extorting

THE LETTER OF THE LAW

A Proposal for Free Airtime for Political Candidates

(a) In General—

  (1) Program Content Requirements—[The] Federal Communications Commission may not determine that a broadcasting station has met its obligation to operate in the public interest unless the station demonstrates to the satisfaction of the Commission that—

    (A) it broadcast at least 2 hours per week of candidate-centered programming or issue-centered programming during each of the 6 weeks preceding a Federal election, including at least 4 of the weeks immediately preceding a general election; and

    (B) not less than 1 hour of such programming was broadcast in each of those weeks during the period beginning at 5:00 P.M. and ending at 11:35 P.M. in the time zone in which the primary broadcast audience for the station is located.

  (2) Night owl Broadcasts not Counted—For purposes of paragraph (1) any such programming broadcast between midnight and 6:00 A.M. in the time zone in which the primary broadcast audience for the station is located shall not be taken into account.

(b) DEFINITIONS—In this section ...

  (2) Candidate-Centered Programming—The term "candidate-centered programming"—

    (A) includes debates, interviews, candidate statements, and other program formats that provide for a discussion of issues by the candidate; but

    (B) does not include paid political advertisements....

  (4) Issue-Centered Programming—The term "issue-centered programming"—

    (A) includes debates, interviews, statements, and other program formats that provide for a discussion of any ballot measure which appears on a ballot in a forthcoming election; but

    (B) does not include paid political advertisements.

Source: Political Campaign Broadcast Activity Improvements Act, S. 3124 § 3, 107th Cong. (2002)

money from political candidates, broadcasters say that they
certainly have not taken advantage of such candidates. In fact,
broadcasters have begrudgingly complied with regulations that
require television stations to give their best possible ad rates to
political candidates. To require stations to actually *give* free
airtime to candidates takes it a step too far.

Broadcasters argue that they already devote a significant
amount of coverage to political campaigns through news stories,
interviews, and debates. Free airtime proposals ignore an
obvious point: Viewers are not really interested in the type of
programming that campaign reformers want to impose on the
public. Broadcasters are in the business of making money and,
therefore, broadcast programming that will attract the most
viewers. If people were interested in political programming, then
broadcasters would carry more of it. The National Association of
Broadcasters (NAB) insists that not all candidates actually want
to participate in debates. A spokesperson for NAB said, "One of
the constant challenges faced by broadcasters is persuading
candidates to actually accept the numerous free air time and
debate offers from local stations."[90]

> • **Should the government be allowed to limit the type of
> programming that television stations carry?**

"Attack ads" may not represent politics at its finest, but civil libertarians believe that restricting them would be even worse. Any ban
on attack ads amounts to government regulation of political
speech and squelches criticism of elected officials—principles that
offend the Constitution. Many are calling upon Congress to keep
out of regulating television, rejecting the idea that the airwaves are
a "public trust," and maintaining that government control of the
media endangers democracy.

The Future
of American
Democracy

Since the controversy surrounding the 2000 presidential election, many people have wondered whether incremental changes in our system of campaigning and voting—such as campaign finance reform and the Help America Vote Act—are enough to preserve our democracy. Some people have called for radical changes to the American system of government.

For example, some people have called for scrapping the Electoral College, which elects the president using representatives chosen from each state. Al Gore won the "popular vote," meaning that more people voted for him than for George W. Bush (even without counting the disputed ballots in Florida and elsewhere). However, because Bush won crucial statewide elections, the Electoral College chose Bush as president. Although many people believe that the system makes little sense, the Electoral College is deeply rooted in the American system of government, in which the founders wanted to ensure that states had a major voice in the federal government.

Most observers believe that it will be difficult to eliminate the Electoral College, and not simply because history is on its side. It is always difficult to change "the system," primarily because the people responsible for changing the laws—elected officials—are the same people who have gained power through the existing system. With its bans on attack ads and limits on party fundraising, the Bipartisan Campaign Reform Act (BCRA) has been called an "incumbency protection" law because it makes it more difficult for challengers to unseat elected officials.

With the constitutionality and effectiveness of recent laws such as the BCRA and the Help America Vote Act very much in doubt, many people fear that it will be "back to the drawing

THE LETTER OF THE LAW

Constitutional Authority for the Electoral College

The Electors shall meet in their respective states and vote by ballot for President and Vice-President, one of whom, at least, shall not be an inhabitant of the same state with themselves; they shall name in their ballots the person voted for as President, and in distinct ballots the person voted for as Vice-President, and they shall make distinct lists of all persons voted for as President, and of all persons voted for as Vice-President, and of the number of votes for each, which lists they shall sign and certify, and transmit sealed to the seat of the government of the United States, directed to the President of the Senate;—the President of the Senate shall, in the presence of the Senate and House of Representatives, open all the certificates and the votes shall then be counted;—The person having the greatest number of votes for President, shall be the President, if such number be a majority of the whole number of Electors appointed; and if no person have such majority, then from the persons having the highest numbers not exceeding three on the list of those voted for as President, the House of Representatives shall choose immediately, by ballot, the President. But in choosing the President, the votes shall be taken by states, the representation from each state having one vote; a quorum for this purpose shall consist of a member or members from two-thirds of the states, and a majority of all the states shall be necessary to a choice.

Source: U.S. Constitution, Amendment XII

board" for reforming the election process. On the other hand, many people are happy with the electoral system the way it is; many politicians benefit from voter apathy, especially when minorities, immigrants, and the poor do not vote.

Despite facing resistance to change, reformers carry on with new initiatives that they hope will help ensure not only every person's opportunity to vote but that also will make it easier to vote and make each person's vote more meaningful. One idea is to hold elections using the Internet, with the goal of dramatically increasing voter participation. However, even if everyone votes, many votes will continue to be "wasted" in our "winner-take-all" system, in which 50.1 percent of the voters in any district elect the candidate of their choice, and the other 49.9 percent of voters have their preferences more or less ignored.

- **Does it make sense that the person who gets the most votes for president doesn't always win?**

Online Elections

One change that many people have suggested is to hold elections over the Internet; in fact, it has been tried in several places. To proponents, it makes perfect sense to use the Internet for voting. Journalist Jeffrey Birnbaum writes: "Surely if we can buy and then register a car over the Internet, we can register to vote and then actually cast a ballot. It only makes sense that we should harness the Internet in ways that will open our democracy to more and more people."[91]

The Arizona Democratic Party experimented with Internet voting during the 2000 presidential primary. The purpose of this election was to choose the party's nominee for president, not to cast any "official" votes for president, which is reserved for the November general election in which all registered voters throughout the nation can participate. However, it was an officially sanctioned election with the option of voting online, and many hope that in the future, such opportunities will continue.

The Arizona primary election demonstrated that the availability of online voting has the potential to greatly increase voter participation, especially among minority voters. According to a press release by *election.com*, which managed the online election:

> The results showed that the minority vote was strengthened significantly by high voter turnout, and in many cases by much more than the overall baseline increase in turnout.

> "I'm pleased that our efforts, in conjunction with *election.com*, to make this the most inclusive, accessible election ever, increased voter turnout by more than 600%," said Mark Fleisher, Chairman of the Arizona Democratic Party. "In comparison to both 1992 and 1996, voter turnout increased significantly in nearly all counties and legislative districts. . . .

> Overall, voter turnout was up 622% over 1996. In the largely Hispanic legislative districts 22 and 23 in Maricopa county, turnout increased by 828% and 1011% respectively. In Apache county, turnout increased by 515% compared to 1996."[92]

However, online voting has strong critics, and it might be years—if ever—before the nation is ready for online general elections. One of the biggest concerns about online election is voter fraud. Arizona required voters to input seven-digit identification numbers that were mailed to registered Democrats before the election. However, there is certainly no good way of verifying that the person entering the identification number is the person to whom it was assigned. Compared to systems in which voters must appear in person and sign a log, the anonymity of Internet voting has even greater potential for fraud. Some people have expressed concern with electronic voting systems that do not maintain a "hard copy" of the votes: If a candidate wanted to challenge the election, there would be no way to do a recount.

• **Do you think that the Internet makes fraud easier?**

The effect of winner-take-all on racial and political minorities.

As the 2000 presidential election demonstrates, nowhere is the phrase "winner-take-all" more appropriate than in American politics. In a national election for president, one person wins and everyone else loses. The same is true of statewide elections for seats in the U.S. Senate and for district elections to the House of Representatives.

Some people have begun to wonder if winner-take-all is the right way to elect representatives. Most states—except for the least populous states, such as North and South Dakota—elect more than one representative. Under the current system, each state electing multiple representatives is divided into congressional districts, each of which elects one representative. In each district, one candidate wins and everyone else loses. Even with a great deal of support statewide, a candidate must win his or her district in order to be elected. Additionally, in a state that is 40 percent Republican, there is no guarantee that 40 percent of the state's representatives will be Republican, because any successful candidate must win more than 50 percent of the vote in his or her district.

Another problem with the current system, in which states are divided into districts that each elect one candidate, is that the district lines are subject to manipulation. Congressional districts change regularly for two reasons: changes in the number of representatives and population shifts within a state. Someone has to draw the new district lines, and that responsibility usually falls to the majority party, which can draw the districts in a way that favors the party. By maximizing the number of districts in which their party has a majority, the party can maximize its number of representatives. Redistricting in a way that gives one party an advantage is commonly known as "gerrymandering," a term that comes from the name of former Massachusetts Governor Elbridge Gerry; the state had an oddly shaped district that looked like a salamander.

- **Do you think that there is any fair way to divide a state into voting districts?**

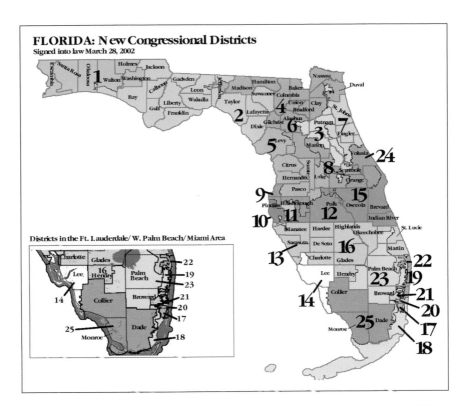

FLORIDA: New Congressional Districts
Signed into law March 28, 2002

Districts in the Ft. Lauderdale/ W. Palm Beach/ Miami Area

This map of Florida shows how the state is broken up into congressional districts, drawn up to correspond to population. Some politicians have supported the idea of drawing political districts in a deliberate attempt to give a new district a minority population, to make the election of minority candidates more likely.

Political science professor Douglas J. Amy explains that there are two techniques for gerrymandering: "cracking" and "packing." [93] Cracking involves splitting a district in which a majority of voters support the other party, thereby relocating voters to districts in which they are the political minority. Packing involves putting as many of the other party's voters as possible into as few districts as possible. Whether the other party controls 51 percent of the votes in a district or 100 percent of the votes in that district, it still gets only one representative.

THE GERRY-MANDER.

The term "gerrymandering" comes from the name of Massachusetts Governor Elbridge Gerry, who served from 1810 to 1812. During his term in office, Gerry drew a bizarre-looking congressional district (seen here) that some people believed looked like either a salamander or a monster.

Therefore, packing voters into districts means that the same number of voters elects fewer representatives.

Though "gerrymandering" has traditionally been a tool for a dominant party to increase its dominance, some have applied the term to efforts to increase the voting power of racial minorities. For a time, in response to rulings by the U.S. Department of Justice, states created congressional districts comprising a majority of African-American voters. For example, when Georgia gained an eleventh congressional district after the 1990 census, the Department of Justice insisted that three of the districts have an African-American majority, reflecting the fact that 27 percent of Georgia's population was African-American. In response, because the state already had two majority-African-American districts, the state legislature created a congressional district that included predominantly African-American sections of Atlanta and Savannah—two cities over 250 miles (402 kilometers) apart—as well as the area in between.

> • **Should it be assumed that white politicians cannot adequately represent African Americans and vice versa?**

However, in a ruling that put strict limits on the ability of states to take race into account when creating legislative districts, the Supreme Court invalidated the district. In *Miller* v. *Johnson,* the Court held:

> The [trial] court found it was "exceedingly obvious" from the shape of the Eleventh District, together with the relevant racial demographics, that the drawing of narrow land bridges to incorporate within the District outlying appendages containing nearly 80 percent of the district's total black population was a deliberate attempt to bring black populations into the district. . . . Although by comparison with other districts the geometric shape of the Eleventh District may not seem bizarre on its face, when its shape is considered in conjunction with its racial and population densities, the story of racial gerrymandering seen by the District Court becomes much clearer. The [trial] had before it considerable additional evidence showing that the General Assembly was motivated by a predominant, overriding desire to assign black populations to the Eleventh District. . . .
>
> Only if our political system and our society cleanse themselves of that discrimination will all members of the polity

share an equal opportunity to gain public office regardless of race. . . . The end is neither assured nor well served, however, by carving electorates into racial blocs. . . . It takes a short-sighted and unauthorized view of the Voting Rights Act to invoke that statute, which has played a decisive role in redressing some of our worst forms of discrimination, to demand the very racial stereotyping the Fourteenth Amendment forbids.[94]

The Court's decision was widely criticized. In his dissent from the majority's decision, Justice John Paul Stevens wrote:

[It is distressing that the Court equates] traditional gerry-manders, designed to maintain or enhance a dominant group's power, with a dominant group's decision to share its power with a previously underrepresented group. In my view, districting plans violate the Equal Protection Clause when they "serve no purpose other than to favor one segment—whether racial, ethnic, religious, economic, or political—that may occupy a position of strength at a particular point in time, or to disadvantage a politically weak segment of the community." . . . In contrast, I do not see how a districting plan that favors a politically weak group can violate equal protection. . . .

The Court's refusal to distinguish an enactment that helps a minority group from enactments that cause it harm is especially unfortunate at the intersection of race and voting, given that African Americans and other disadvantaged groups have struggled so long and so hard for inclusion in that most central exercise of our democracy.[95]

• **Do you support affirmative action?**

Under the current winner-take-all system, it is difficult for both racial minorities and minority political parties to gain a share of political power. To remedy this perceived unfairness, some people have called for abandoning the current system in favor of "proportional representation." Under such a system, the state's voters would not be divided into single-representative districts, but instead each district (or the entire state) would elect multiple representatives. Professor Amy recommends that each district elect at least five seats.[96] In a five-candidate district, the top five candidates would win; therefore, a candidate would need to attract just over 20 percent of the vote, rather than more than 50 percent of the vote, to ensure victory. With proportional representation, minority groups could more easily elect a candidate of their choice. Although common in Europe, proportional representation represents a significant change from current American politics, and remains a long-term objective for its supporters.

Since the 2000 presidential election, in which many people either could not vote or had their ballots discarded, Congress has enacted significant legislation reforming the electoral process. However, many people think that further reforms are needed to ensure that each citizen has a voice in politics. Some have suggested that Internet elections could increase the number of people who vote, but critics worry about fraud. A long-term solution might be a system of proportional representation that would give more of a voice to political and racial minorities.

Voting: The Cornerstone of Democracy?

1 U.S. Commission on Civil Rights, *Voting Irregularities in Florida During the 2000 Presidential Election* (August 2002). Available online at http://www.usccr.gov/.

2 Ibid.

3 *Bush* v. *Gore*, No. 00-949 (December 12, 2000) (per curiam).

4 Neal Peirce, "Taming 'Winner Take All' — A Cure for All Elections Malaise," *Stateline.org*, September 18, 2002.

Point: Voter Rights Laws Should Be Strengthened to Ensure That Each Citizen Has a Meaningful Vote

5 Memorandum from A. Rosen to Mr. Belmont (September 18, 1964). Part of the Federal Bureau of Investigation's online FOIA reading room at http://foia.fbi.gov

6 2 U.S.C. § 1973 (2000).

7 42 U.S.C. § 1973-gg (2000).

8 Pub. L. No. 107-252, 116 Stat. 1666 (2002).

9 U.S. Commission on Civil Rights, *Voting Irregularities in Florida During the 2000 Presidential Election* (August 2002). Available online at http://www.usccr.gov/.

10 Ibid.

11 Congressional Record E220 (February 27, 2001).

12 National Council of La Raza, *Mobilizing the Vote: Latinos and Immigrants in the 2002 Midterm Election* (November 2002). Available online at http://www.nclr.org/.

13 Congressional Record E220 (February 27, 2001).

14 U.S. Commission on Civil Rights, *Voting Irregularities in Florida During the 2000 Presidential Election* (August 2002). Available online at http://www.usccr.gov/.

15 Congressional Record S1228 (February 27, 2002).

16 Press Release, National Council of La Raza, "NCLR Urges Congress to Vote No on the Help America Vote Act" (October 9, 2002).

17 Ibid.

Counterpoint: Measures Are Needed to Prevent Manipulation of Elections and Voter Fraud

18 Kathleen Wereszynski, "Stunt Reveals Holes in 'Motor Voter' Law," *foxnews.com*, June 17, 2001.

19 Jonah Goldberg, "Vote.com: The Perils of 'Cyber-Democracy,'" *National Review Online*, December 20, 1999.

20 Byron York, "Bad Lands, Bad Votes," *National Review Online*, December 19, 2002.

21 Ibid.

22 Jim Boulet, Jr., "Will Non-citizens Decide the Election?" *National Review Online*, November 10, 2000.

23 U.S. Commission on Civil Rights, *Voting Irregularities in Florida During the 2000 Presidential Election*, August 2002. (Dissenting statement by Commissioners Thernstrom and Redenbaugh.) Available online at http://www.usccr.gov/.

24 Ibid.

25 Congressional Record S1224 (February 27, 2002).

26 *Hearings on the Motor Voter Act and Voter Fraud Before the before the Committee of Rules and Administration of the Senate*, 107th Congress (2001) (statement of John Samples).

27 Ibid.

28 Ibid.

29 Congressional Record S1224 (February 27, 2002).

30 Robert Pear, "Bush Signs Law Intended to End Disputes," *The New York Times*, October 29, 2002.

31 Ibid.

Point: Money Is Corrupting American Democracy

32 Kathleen Murphy, "Govs' Races Break the Bank," *Stateline.org*, November 11, 2002.

33 Pub. L. No. 107-155 § 307 (March 27, 2002) (amending limit to $2,000); 2 U.S.C. § 441a (2000) (setting limit at $1,000).

34 Pub. L. No. 107-155 § 307 (March 27, 2002) (extending ban to cover political parties); 2 U.S.C. § 441b (2000) (banning most contributions by corporations and labor unions).

35 Russell D. Feingold, "Representative
Democracy versus Corporate Democracy:
How Soft Money Erodes the Principle
of "One Person, One Vote," in Annelise
Anderson, ed., *Political Money: Deregulating American Politics* (Stanford, CA:
Hoover Institution Press, 2000), p. 317.
36 147 Congressional Record S2434
(March 19, 2001).
37 Brief for Committee for Economic
Development, *McConnell* v. *FEC*
(Dist. D.C.) (No. 02-0582).
38 Ibid.
39 Ibid.
40 147 Congressional Record S2434
(March 19, 2001).
41 Brief for Committee for Economic
Development, *McConnell* v. *FEC*
(Dist. D.C.) (No. 02-0582)..
42 Jay Reeves, "N.Y. Dollars Key in District
7 Race," *Montgomery Advertiser*, June 27,
2002.
43 Jonathan Rosenblum, "Payback
Time for New York Jews," *Hamodia*,
September 6, 2002. Available online at
http://www.jewishmediaresources.com.
44 Thomas B. Edsall, "Impact of McKinney
Loss Worries Some Democrats: Tension
Between Blacks, Jews a Concern,"
Washington Post, August 22, 2002, p. A4.
45 147 Congressional Record S2436
(March 19, 2001).
46 Brief for former leaders of ACLU,
McConnell v. *FEC* (Dist. D.C.)
(No. 02-0582).

**Counterpoint: Campaign Contributions
Are a Vital Part of the Democratic
Process**
47 Tom Bethell, "The Money Chase,"
in Annelise Anderson, ed., *Political
Money: Deregulating American Politics*
(Stanford, CA: Hoover Institution
Press, 2000), p. 251.
48 Ibid.
49 Doug Bandow, "Best Reform is No
Limits," *USA Today*, August 11, 2000.
50 Steven E. Schier, "One Cheer for Soft
Money," in Christopher Luna, ed.,
Campaign Finance Reform (New York:
H.W. Wilson Company, 2001), pp. 90, 92.
51 Ibid., pp. 91, 93.

52 Russell D. Feingold, "Representative
Democracy versus Corporate Democracy:
How Soft Money Erodes the Principle
of "One Person, One Vote," in Annelise
Anderson, ed., *Political Money: Deregu-
lating American Politics* (Stanford, CA:
Hoover Institution Press, 2000), p. 317.
53 Allison R. Hayward, " 'Conservative'
Campaign-Finance Reform?" *National
Review Online*, September 14, 2000.
54 John Samples, " 'Soft Money' Aids
Democracy," *USA Today*, September 29,
2000.
55 Ibid.
56 Doug Bandow, "Best Reform is No
Limits," *USA Today*, August 11, 2000.
57 Tom Bethell, "The Money Chase," in
Annelise Anderson, ed., *Political Money:
Deregulating American Politics* (Stanford,
CA: Hoover Institution Press, 2000),
p. 251.
58 Signing statement, President George W.
Bush, Bipartisan Campaign Reform Act
of 2002, March 27, 2002.
59 Michael Barone, "Lessons from Rep.
Cynthia McKinney's Defeat," *U.S. News
and World Report*, online edition,
August 29, 2002.
60 Erik S. Jaffe and Robert A. Levy,
"Real Campaign Reform," *Regulation*,
Fall 2002, p. 8.
61 Brief for Institute for Justice and Cato
Institute, *McConnell* v. *FEC* (Dist. D.C.)
(No. 02-0582).

**Point: The Government Should
Regulate Television Advertisements and Campaign Coverage**
62 Darrell M. West, *Checkbook Democracy:
How Money Corrupts Political Campaigns*
(Boston: Northeastern University Press,
2000), p. 30.
63 Mike Denison, "Taylor Quits Senate Race,"
Great Falls Tribune, October 11, 2002.
64 Ibid.
65 424 U.S. 1 (1976) (per curiam).
66 Brief for former leaders of ACLU,
McConnell v. *FEC* (Dist. D.C.)
(No. 02-0582).
67 Ibid.
68 Bipartisan Campaign Reform Act, Pub.
L. No. 107-155 (March 22, 2002).

69 Congressional Record S10585 (October 16, 2002).
70 Jeffrey H. Birnbaum, *The Money Men: The Real Story of Fund-raising's Influence on Political Power in America* (New York: Crown Publishers, 2000), pp. 261–262.
71 Ibid., p. 262.
72 Congressional Record S10585-86 (October 16, 2002).
73 Congressional Record S10583 (October 16, 2002).
74 Congressional Record S10585 (October 16, 2002).
75 Congressional Record S10583 (October 16, 2002).
76 Ric Bainter and Paul Lhevine, "Political Reform Comes From Communities," in Christopher Luna, ed., *Campaign Finance Reform* (New York: H.W. Wilson Company, 2001), p. 167. Originally published in *National Civic Review*, Spring 1998.

Counterpoint: Government Restrictions on Television Advertisements and Programming Are Unconstitutional and Undemocratic
77 Brief for National Rifle Association, *McConnell* v. *FEC* (Dist. D.C.) (No. 02-0582).
78 Ibid.
79 Brief for Media Institute, *McConnell* v. *FEC* (Dist. D.C.) (No. 02-0582).
80 Lillian R. BeVier, *Campaign Finance "Reform" Proposals: A First Amendment Analysis, Cato Policy Analysis No. 282* (Washington, D.C.: Cato Institute, 1997).
81 *New York Times Co.* v. *Sullivan*, 376 U.S. 254 (1964).
82 Brief for ACLU, *McConnell* v. *FEC* (Dist. D.C.) (No. 02-0582).
83 Ibid.

84 424 U.S. 1 (1976) (per curiam).
85 Erik S. Jaffe and Robert A. Levy, "Real Campaign Reform," *Regulation*, Fall 2002.
86 Brief for ACLU, *McConnell* v. *FEC* (Dist. D.C.) (No. 02-0582).
87 Bradley A. Smith, *Unfree Speech: The Folly of Campaign Finance Reform* (Princeton, NJ: Princeton University Press, 2001), p. 96.
88 Pete du Pont, "Price Controls on Democracy," in Annelise Anderson, ed., *Political Money: Deregulating American Politics* (Stanford, CA: Hoover Institution Press, 2000), p. 280.
89 Edward H. Crane, "The Case Against Free Radio and Television Time for Politicians," *Cato Daily News*, February 20, 1996.
90 Reporters Committee for Freedom of the Press, "Campaign Reform Threatens Broadcasters' Rights," *News Media and the Law*, 26 No. 3 (Summer 2002).

The Future of American Democracy
91 Jeffrey H. Birnbaum, *The Money Men: The Real Story of Fund-raising's Influence on Political Power in America* (New York: Crown Publishers, 2000), p. 270.
92 Press release, *election.com*, March 24, 2000.
93 Douglas J. Amy, *Real Choices/New Voices: How Proportional Representation Could Revitalize American Democracy* (New York: Columbia University Press, 1995).
94 *Miller* v. *Johnson*, 515 U.S. 900 (1995).
95 *Miller* v. *Johnson*, 515 U.S. 900 (1995) (Stevens, J., dissenting).
96 Douglas J. Amy, *Real Choices/New Voices: How Proportional Representation Could Revitalize American Democracy* (New York: Columbia University Press, 1995).

General

Anderson, Annelise, ed. *Political Money: Deregulating American Politics.* Stanford, CA: Hoover Institution Press, 2000.

Cohen, Joshua, and Joel Rogers, eds. *Money and Politics: Financing Our Elections Democratically.* Boston: Beacon Press, 1999.

Federal Election Commission
www.fec.gov
Federal agency overseeing campaigns and elections. Text of federal election laws and regulations and information about candidates' sources of funding.

Luna, Christopher, ed. *Campaign Finance Reform.* New York: H.W. Wilson Company, 2001.

Against Regulation of Elections

Cato Institute
www.cato.org
Libertarian "think tank" opposing unnecessary government regulations. Extensive information about arguments against campaign reforms and media regulations.

Media Institute
www.mediainstitute.org
Nonprofit organization specializing in First Amendment issues. Provides arguments against government regulation of advertising and broadcasting.

National Association of Broadcasters
www.nab.org
Association of radio and television broadcasters. Opposes restrictions on broadcasters.

Smith, Bradley A. *Unfree Speech: The Folly of Campaign Finance Reform.* Princeton, NJ: Princeton University Press, 2001.

Favoring Regulation of Elections

Birnbaum, Jeffrey H. *The Money Men: The Real Story of Fund-raising's Influence on Political Power in America.* New York: Crown Publishers, 2000.

Common Cause
www.commoncause.org
National membership organization dedicated to increasing accountability of elected officials and reducing the impact of money on politics.

Democracy 21
www.democracy21.org
Nonprofit organization seeking to reduce the influence of money on politics.

Other Resources

Campaign and Media Legal Center

www.camlc.org

Nonprofit legal group representing the "public interest" in campaign finance and media law cases. Extensive information about ongoing litigation.

Center for Representative Politics

www.opensecrets.org

Divulges sources of campaign financing, with analysis of controversial contributions, such as those by Enron.

Center for Voting and Democracy

www.fairvote.org

In-depth information about proportional representation, redistricting, and instant-runoff voting.

League of Women Voters

www.lwv.org

National membership organization devoted to increasing citizen participation in politics. Extensive information about election and campaign finance reform.

West, Darrell M. *Checkbook Democracy: How Money Corrupts Political Campaigns.* Boston: Northeastern University Press, 2000.

Legislation and Case Law

New York Times Co. v. *Sullivan* , 376 U.S. 254 (1964)
> Held that a public official cannot collect libel damages for inaccurate statements without demonstrating "actual malice."

Voting Rights Act, 42 U.S.C. § 1973.
> Outlawed tactics used to disenfranchise minority voters, such as poll taxes, literacy tests, and character tests.

Red Lion Broadcasting Co. v. *FCC*, 395 U.S. 367 (1969)
> Held that the government can require broadcasters to act in the public interest because they use the public airwaves.

Buckley v. *Valeo*, 424 U.S. 1 (1976) (per curiam).
> Held that the government can regulate campaign contributions more closely than it can regulate other forms of political expression.

National Voter Registration Act, 42 U.S.C. §§ 1973gg
> Commonly called "Motor Voter" law; requires states to provide voter registration opportunities at motor vehicle bureaus and other public offices.

Nixon v. *Shrink Missouri PAC*, No. 98-963 (January 24, 2000)
> Upheld Missouri's limit on campaign contributions.

Bush v. *Gore*, No. 00-949 (Dec. 12, 2000) (per curiam).
> Ended Florida's recount of ballots in the 2000 presidential election.

Bipartisan Campaign Reform Act, Pub. L. No. 107-155 (March 22, 2002).
> Outlawed "soft money" contributions to political parties; placed stricter limits on campaign advertising.

Help America Vote Act, 42 U.S.C. § 15483
> Mandated "provisional balloting" so that nobody is turned away from the polls; imposed identification requirements for voting.

Concepts and Standards

Electoral College
disenfranchisement
voter error
intent of the voter
poll tax
discrimination
disproportionate effect
provisional balloting
civil disobedience
voting rights
partisan politics
voter fraud
campaign finance reform
campaign contributions

soft money
bribery
corruption
free speech
political parties
attack ads
sham issue ads
public interest
broadcast spectrum
free airtime
candidate-centered programming
issue-centered programming
winner-take-all
proportional representation

Beginning Legal Research

The goal of POINT/COUNTERPOINT is not only to provide the reader with an introduction to a controversial issue affecting society, but also to encourage the reader to explore the issue more fully. This appendix, then, is meant to serve as a guide to the reader in researching the current state of the law as well as exploring some of the public-policy arguments as to why existing laws should be changed or new laws are needed.

Like many types of research, legal research has become much faster and more accessible with the invention of the Internet. This appendix discusses some of the best starting points, but of course "surfing the Net" will uncover endless additional sources of information—some more reliable than others. Some important sources of law are not yet available on the Internet, but these can generally be found at the larger public and university libraries. Librarians usually are happy to point patrons in the right direction.

The most important source of law in the United States is the Constitution. Originally enacted in 1787, the Constitution outlines the structure of our federal government and sets limits on the types of laws that the federal government and state governments can pass. Through the centuries, a number of amendments have been added to or changed in the Constitution, most notably the first ten amendments, known collectively as the Bill of Rights, which guarantee important civil liberties. Each state also has its own constitution, many of which are similar to the U.S. Constitution. It is important to be familiar with the U.S. Constitution because so many of our laws are affected by its requirements. State constitutions often provide protections of individual rights that are even stronger than those set forth in the U.S. Constitution.

Within the guidelines of the U.S. Constitution, Congress—both the House of Representatives and the Senate—passes bills that are either vetoed or signed into law by the President. After the passage of the law, it becomes part of the United States Code, which is the official compilation of federal laws. The state legislatures use a similar process, in which bills become law when signed by the state's governor. Each state has its own official set of laws, some of which are published by the state and some of which are published by commercial publishers. The U.S. Code and the state codes are an important source of legal research; generally, legislators make efforts to make the language of the law as clear as possible.

However, reading the text of a federal or state law generally provides only part of the picture. In the American system of government, after the legislature passes laws and the executive (U.S. President or state governor) signs them, it is up to the judicial branch of the government, the court system, to interpret the laws and decide whether they violate any provision of the Constitution. At the state level, each state's supreme court has the ultimate authority in determining what a law means and whether or not it violates the state constitution. However, the federal courts—headed by the U.S. Supreme Court—can review state laws and court decisions to determine whether they violate federal laws or the U.S. Constitution. For example, a state court may find that a particular criminal law is valid under the state's constitution, but a federal court may then review the state court's decision and determine that the law is invalid under the U.S. Constitution.

It is important, then, to read court decisions when doing legal research. The Constitution uses language that is intentionally very general—for example, prohibiting "unreasonable searches and seizures" by the police—and court cases often provide more guidance. For example, the U.S. Supreme Court's 2001 decision in *Kyllo v. United States* held that scanning the outside of a person's house using a heat sensor to determine whether the person is growing marijuana is unreasonable—*if* it is done without a search warrant secured from a judge. Supreme Court decisions provide the most definitive explanation of the law of the land, and it is therefore important to include these in research. Often, when the Supreme Court has not decided a case on a particular issue, a decision by a federal appeals court or a state supreme court can provide guidance; but just as laws and constitutions can vary from state to state, so can federal courts be split on a particular interpretation of federal law or the U.S. Constitution. For example, federal appeals courts in Louisiana and California may reach opposite conclusions in similar cases.

Lawyers and courts refer to statutes and court decisions through a formal system of citations. Use of these citations reveals which court made the decision (or which legislature passed the statute) and when and enables the reader to locate the statute or court case quickly in a law library. For example, the legendary Supreme Court case *Brown v. Board of Education* has the legal citation 347 U.S. 483 (1954). At a law library, this 1954 decision can be found on page 483 of volume 347 of the U.S. Reports, the official collection of the Supreme Court's decisions. Citations can also be helpful in locating court cases on the Internet.

Understanding the current state of the law leads only to a partial under-standing of the issues covered by the POINT/COUNTERPOINT series. For a fuller understanding of the issues, it is necessary to look at public-policy arguments that the current state of the law is not adequately addressing the issue. Many groups lobby for new legislation or changes to existing legislation; the National Rifle Association (NRA), for example, lobbies Congress and the state legislatures constantly to make existing gun control laws less restrictive and not to pass additional laws. The NRA and other groups dedicated to various causes might also intervene in pending court cases: a group such as Planned Parenthood might file a brief *amicus curiae* (as "a friend of the court")—called an "amicus brief"—in a lawsuit that could affect abortion rights. Interest groups also use the media to influence public opinion, issuing press releases and frequently appearing in interviews on news programs and talk shows. The books in POINT/COUNTERPOINT list some of the interest groups that are active in the issue at hand, but in each case there are countless other groups working at the local, state, and national levels. It is important to read everything with a critical eye, for sometimes interest groups present information in a way that can be read only to their advantage. The informed reader must always look for bias.

Finding sources of legal information on the Internet is relatively simple thanks to "portal" sites such as FindLaw (*www.findlaw.com*), which provides access to a variety of constitutions, statutes, court opinions, law review articles, news articles, and other resources—including all Supreme Court decisions issued since 1893. Other useful sources of information include the U.S. Government Printing Office (*www.gpo.gov*), which contains a complete copy of the U.S. Code, and the Library of Congress's THOMAS system (*thomas.loc.gov*), which offers access to bills pending before Congress as well as recently passed laws. Of course, the Internet changes every second of every day, so it is best to do some independent searching. Most cases, studies, and opinions that are cited or referred to in public debate can be found online— and *everything* can be found in one library or another.

The Internet can provide a basic understanding of most important legal issues, but not all sources can be found there. To find some documents it is necessary to visit the law library of a university or a public law library; some cities have public law libraries, and many library systems keep legal documents at the main branch. On the following page are some common citation forms.

COMMON CITATION FORMS

Source of Law	Sample Citation	Notes
U.S. Supreme Court	*Employment Division* v. *Smith*, 485 U.S. 660 (1988)	The U.S. Reports is the official record of Supreme Court decisions. There is also an unofficial Supreme Court ("S.Ct.") reporter.
U.S. Court of Appeals	*United States* v. *Lambert*, 695 F.2d 536 (11th Cir.1983)	Appellate cases appear in the Federal Reporter, designated by "F." The 11th Circuit has jurisdiction in Alabama, Florida, and Georgia.
U.S. District Court	*Carillon Importers, Ltd.* v. *Frank Pesce Group, Inc.*, 913 F.Supp. 1559 (S.D.Fla.1996)	Federal trial-level decisions are reported in the Federal Supplement ("F.Supp."). Some states have multiple federal districts; this case originated in the Southern District of Florida.
U.S. Code	Thomas Jefferson Commemoration Commission Act, 36 U.S.C., §149 (2002)	Sometimes the popular names of legislation—names with which the public may be familiar—are included with the U.S. Code citation.
State Supreme Court	*Sterling* v. *Cupp*, 290 Ore. 611, 614, 625 P.2d 123, 126 (1981)	The Oregon Supreme Court decision is reported in both the state's reporter and the Pacific regional reporter.
State statute	Pennsylvania Abortion Control Act of 1982, 18 Pa. Cons. Stat. 3203-3220 (1990)	States use many different citation formats for their statutes.

page:

14: Associated Press, AP/Gary I. Rothstein

18: Data compiled from the Federal Election Commission

22: Associated Press, AP

27: US Census Bureau, *Voting and Registration in the Election of November 2000*

36: Associated Press, AP/Mike Wintroath

49: Courtesy Center for Responsive Politics, *www.opensecrets.com*

53: Courtesy Center for Responsive Politics, *www.opensecrets.com*

57: Reprinted with special permission of King Features Syndicate

69: Associated Press, AP/Janet Hostetter

72: National Election Studies

75: © David J. And Janice L. Frent/ CORBIS

79: Associated Press, Davis for Governor Campaign

95: Associated Press, AP

103: National Committee for an Effective Congress (NCEC)

104: © Bettmann/CORBIS

Cover: Associated Press, AP/Amy E. Conn

ALAN MARZILLI, of Durham, North Carolina, is an independent consultant working on several ongoing projects for state and federal government agencies and nonprofit organizations. He has spoken about mental health issues in more than 20 states, the District of Columbia, and Puerto Rico; his work includes training mental health administrators, nonprofit management and staff, and people with mental illness and their family members on a wide variety of topics, including effective advocacy, community-based mental health services, and housing. He has written several handbooks and training curricula that are used nationally. He managed statewide and national mental health advocacy programs and worked for several public interest lobbying organizations in Washington, D.C. while studying law at Georgetown University.